Anti-Inflammatory Cookbook for Beginners

Easy and Affordable Recipes for Reducing Inflammation, Increasing Energy, and Supporting Immune Health

Rosa James

All images in this cookbook were thoughtfully crafted using AI technology to best represent each recipe as accurately as possible. While every effort has been made to ensure these images reflect the results you can achieve in your kitchen, please note that slight variations may occur based on individual ingredients, tools, and techniques.

We hope these visuals inspire and guide you as you create delicious meals. Enjoy cooking and making these recipes your own!

Table of Contents

Introduction

Can you imagine waking up each morning feeling refreshed, full of energy, and ready to embrace the day? Imagine meals that not only satiate your hunger but also nurture your body and soul. I'm talking about dishes adorned with a rainbow of vibrant colors, bursting with flavors that dance on your tongue. That is the transformative power of embracing an anti-inflammatory diet.

Hi, I'm Rosa James, and I'm here to take you on a journey to better health through healthier, more specific food choices. When we embrace the anti-inflammatory diet, food morphs from mere sustenance into a powerful ally in achieving optimal health and vitality. In this book, I'll guide you through the delicious world of anti-inflammatory foods, offering not just recipes, but a blueprint for a healthier lifestyle, and better yet, we'll have fun doing it too!

In today's fast-paced world, convenience often trumps nutrition, many of us find ourselves caught in the cycle of inflammation—an underlying culprit behind numerous chronic ailments. From joint pain to digestive issues, fatigue to skin problems, inflammation can wreak havoc on our bodies, often silently and insidiously. But there is hope, and it lies within the food we eat.

An anti-inflammatory diet focuses on consuming natural, wholesome ingredients that fight inflammation while nourishing every cell in your body. These aren't restrictive or bland meals, but rather vibrant, flavor-packed dishes that bring joy to your plate and revitalization to your life.

Our journey begins with breakfast, setting the tone for our day with recipes that fuel our morning with nutrients and delight. Whether you are someone who cherishes a leisurely breakfast or races against time every morning, I'll offer options that cater to all lifestyles.

As we navigate through the day, lunchtime brings an opportunity to recharge with meals crafted not just for their nutritional prowess but also for their taste and simplicity. Dinner will become an event to look forward to, a time to unwind and savor meals that soothe our bodies and minds. Food becomes about more than just eating; my recipes are about indulging in the art of cooking and the pleasure of sharing meals with loved ones.

For the moments in between, I also have a selection of snack recipes, opportunities to nourish rather than nibble mindlessly, keeping cravings at bay, and our energy levels high to spur us forward.

For those with a sweet tooth, desserts in an anti-inflammatory diet aren't about deprivation. Instead, they celebrate nature's bounty. When the craving strikes for a comforting warm beverage or a refreshing cool drink, our teas and smoothies provide a delightful finish, packed with antioxidants and flavor.

This is more than just a cookbook. It's an invitation to rethink your relationship with food, to explore and experiment, to engage your senses, and rediscover the pleasures of eating well. As you dive into these pages, allow curiosity to guide you and remember that each small step brings you closer to improved health and well-being.

So, are you ready? Ready to discover the sumptuous, healing potential packed into every meal you create? Ready to embark on a culinary adventure that will transform not just your diet, but your entire lifestyle?

Welcome to the anti-inflammatory diet, where each meal is a celebration of life and each dish a testament to the power of positive change. Here's to the beginning of a journey toward a healthier, happier you.

Chapter 1:

Understanding Anti-Inflammatory Foods

Gaining an understanding of anti-inflammatory foods is about discovering how certain foods can significantly impact our health and well-being. These foods, revered for their natural health-enhancing properties, can help bridge the gap between a lifestyle plagued by chronic ailments and one that is vibrant and energetic. Introducing these foods into daily life isn't just a trend; it's about choosing ingredients that work harmoniously with our bodies to curb inflammation—an underlying cause of many modern diseases. As we stand at the intersection of diet and disease prevention, this chapter invites you to explore the profound effects that these powerhouse foods can have on our overall health.

Within this chapter, we'll explore which foods play key roles in an anti-inflammatory diet and learn how they contribute to reducing inflammation. We'll venture beyond leafy greens, berries, and fatty fish to examine other critical elements like whole grains, nuts, seeds, and even spices that can transform our meals. We will also look at practical ways to seamlessly weave these beneficial foods into our daily routines through simple meal suggestions and clever substitutions.

We'll also scrutinize some common foods to avoid due to their inflammatory nature, offering guidance to make conscientious eating choices. Step one of our journey will not only highlight the diverse benefits linked to an anti-inflammatory diet but will also encourage a shift toward intentional eating habits that nourish both the body and mind.

Anti-Inflammatory Powerhouses

By selecting the right foods, we can provide our bodies with valuable nutrients and actively reduce the inflammatory processes linked to various chronic illnesses. Among the top candidates for an anti-inflammatory diet are leafy greens such as spinach and kale, berries like blueberries and strawberries, and fatty fish including salmon and mackerel. Therefore, it will come as no surprise that these are the powerhouses we are starting our journey with!

Leafy Greens

Leafy greens are packed with vitamins and antioxidants. Spinach and kale, in particular, are rich in vitamins A, C, and K. These nutrients are crucial for maintaining bodily functions and have strong antioxidant properties which help neutralize harmful free radicals. Vitamin A is vital for vision, immune function, and reproduction, while vitamin C is known for its role in collagen synthesis and immune defense. Vitamin K plays a significant role in blood clotting and bone health. Together, these vitamins contribute to reducing inflammation by protecting cells from damage.

In addition to their vitamin content, leafy greens contain other phytochemicals that enhance their anti-inflammatory effects. For example, chlorophyll, the green pigment in these vegetables, offers detoxifying benefits and supports liver health, thereby aiding in minimizing inflammation. Regularly incorporating leafy greens into meals, whether through salads, smoothies, or cooked dishes, ensures a consistent intake of these beneficial compounds.

Berries

Berries, another important component of an anti-inflammatory diet, are loaded with flavonoids, specifically anthocyanins, which give them their vibrant colors. Blueberries and strawberries are excellent examples of berries that combat oxidative stress—a significant contributor to inflammation. Oxidative stress happens when there's a lack of balance between the antioxidants and free radicals in our bodies, resulting in cellular damage. Consuming berries helps restore this balance, thanks to their high levels of antioxidants that scavenge free radicals.

Research has shown that the regular consumption of berries can significantly lower markers of inflammation (Wartenberg & Spritzler, 2023). Their polyphenolic compounds not only protect the body at the cellular level but also influence gene expression and signal transduction pathways related to inflammation. Incorporating fresh or frozen berries into diets, whether in breakfast bowls, desserts, or as snacks, can be a delicious way to harness their health benefits.

Fatty Fish

Fatty fish, such as salmon and mackerel, are renowned for being rich sources of omega-3 fatty acids, particularly eicosapentaenoic acid (EPA) and docosahexaenoic acid (DHA). These essential fats are known for their potent anti-inflammatory effects. Unlike other fats, omega-3s work to suppress the production of inflammation-stimulating molecules and cytokines within cells. Studies have demonstrated that diets rich in omega-3 fatty acids can lead to reduced expression of inflammatory genes, thus lowering inflammatory markers throughout the body (Rath, 2022).

Beyond inflammation reduction, omega-3 fatty acids support cardiovascular health by helping maintain heart rhythm, reducing triglyceride levels, and lowering blood pressure. They are also crucial for brain health, contributing to cognitive function and potentially reducing the risk of neurodegenerative diseases. Adding fatty fish to meals several times a week can significantly benefit those aiming to follow an anti-inflammatory diet.

To seamlessly incorporate these anti-inflammatory foods into daily life, it's helpful to consider practical guidelines. Aim to regularly include a mix of these foods in various forms—think fresh salads sprinkled with berries, omelets loaded with sautéed spinach and kale, or grilled salmon served with a side of roasted vegetables. Not only does this approach provide diversity in flavor and texture, but it also ensures a broad spectrum of nutrients.

Whole Grains, Nuts, and Seeds

Whole grains, nuts, and seeds are other integral components of an anti-inflammatory diet. These foods offer an array of health benefits that contribute to reducing inflammation and promoting overall well-being. Let's explore!

Whole Grains

Whole grains like brown rice and quinoa are absolute powerhouses of nutrition. They stand out primarily for their high fiber content. Fiber plays a crucial role in aiding digestion by keeping the digestive system functioning smoothly and regularly. This is particularly important because good digestive health is closely linked to reduced inflammation. When digestion is efficient, it minimizes the chances of chronic inflammation markers arising from digestive disorders.

Additionally, whole grains provide essential vitamins and minerals, alongside antioxidants that work together to combat inflammation. They do this by neutralizing free radicals, which can cause cell damage and lead to inflammatory conditions. Studies have shown that diets rich in whole grains can lower the risk of many chronic diseases associated with inflammation, such as type 2 diabetes and heart disease (Milesi et al., 2022).

Nuts

Nuts, especially almonds and walnuts, are another excellent example of nature's gifts that help fight inflammation. They contain healthy fats, primarily monounsaturated and polyunsaturated fats, which are known to reduce bad cholesterol levels and lower heart disease risk. The presence of vitamin E in nuts acts as a potent antioxidant, making their consumption vital in the body's defense against oxidative stress—a key factor in inflammation. By including nuts in your diet, you are adding a layer of protection against inflammation-related illnesses.

Walnuts, in particular, are rich in omega-3 fatty acids, which have been extensively researched for their ability to decrease inflammation and improve cardiovascular health. Incorporating a small handful of nuts into your daily diet can be a delicious and easy way to benefit from their anti-inflammatory properties.

Seeds

Seeds, such as chia and flaxseeds, are tiny but mighty when it comes to their nutritional profile. They boast high levels of lignans (plant compounds that possess antioxidant qualities, helping to reduce inflammation and prevent some types of cancer) and fiber, both of which support anti-inflammatory processes. The fiber in seeds also helps regulate bowel movements and supports gut health, indirectly lowering inflammation risks.

Flaxseeds, specifically, are renowned for their omega-3 content, similar to that found in fatty fish. These essential fats help manage inflammation by balancing the ratio of omega-6 to omega-3 fatty acids in the body—a crucial aspect since a higher intake of omega-6 fatty acids can promote inflammation if not balanced with omega-3s. Including a sprinkle of seeds in your salads, smoothies, or oatmeal can transform them into powerful anti-inflammatory meals.

Combining these foods—leafy greens, berries, fatty fish, whole grains, nuts, and seeds—in our diets can create a synergistic effect in fighting inflammation. For instance, a breakfast bowl featuring quinoa, topped with sliced almonds and flaxseeds, not only provides a hearty start to the day but also loads us up with nutrients that keep inflammation at bay while supporting a balanced diet, which is necessary for maintaining long-term health and preventing inflammation-related diseases.

It is recommended that we gradually increase the intake of these foods to observe significant improvements in inflammation markers over time. The cumulative effects of integrating them into our daily diets can lead to improved health outcomes.

Beyond individual health benefits, incorporating these foods into our diets also contributes to better dietary habits as a whole. They encourage a move away from refined grains, saturated fats, and processed foods, which can aggravate inflammation.

Herbs and Spices

Herbs and spices have played a vital role in culinary traditions across the globe, not just for their ability to enhance flavors but also for their promising health benefits. Among these benefits, their potential role in reducing inflammation is gaining significant attention.

Therefore, it will come as no surprise that we're going to examine a few of them under the metaphorical microscope!

Turmeric

Turmeric stands out as one of the most notable examples of anti-inflammatory spices. This golden-hued spice contains curcumin, a bioactive compound renowned for its powerful anti-inflammatory and antioxidant properties. Curcumin works by blocking inflammatory pathways in the body, thereby helping to prevent and treat inflammation-related conditions. Despite being relatively low in bioavailability, meaning the body does not absorb it very efficiently on its own, curcumin can be enhanced with black pepper. Piperine, an active component in black pepper, increases curcumin's absorption, making turmeric more effective when consumed together. Adding turmeric to curries, soups, or even tea can be a simple yet potent way to harness its benefits.

Ginger

Known for its warm and zesty flavor, ginger has been used in traditional medicine systems for centuries. Scientific research supports ginger's effectiveness as an anti-inflammatory agent, primarily because it inhibits the synthesis of pro-inflammatory cytokines and prostaglandins, the substances in the body that promote inflammation (Mashhadi et al., 2013). Regular consumption of ginger may help manage chronic inflammatory conditions such as arthritis. Whether added to stir-fries, smoothies, or brewed in tea, ginger provides both flavor and healthful qualities, making it a versatile addition to any diet.

Cinnamon

Cinnamon, known for its sweet and woody aroma, is packed with antioxidants like cinnamaldehyde, which helps reduce inflammation by inhibiting the release of inflammation-causing molecules. Including cinnamon in your diet can also contribute to better regulation of blood sugar levels, which is beneficial since imbalanced blood sugar can lead to inflammatory responses in the body. Try sprinkling cinnamon on oatmeal or yogurt for a healthful kick-start to your day!

Cloves

Cloves are tiny, aromatic flower buds that pack a powerful punch against inflammation. Rich in eugenol, a natural anti-inflammatory compound, cloves have been shown to reduce oxidative stress and inhibit the activity of several inflammatory enzymes. These properties make cloves a valuable spice in managing inflammatory conditions. Their distinct flavor pairs well with both sweet and savory dishes, making them a fantastic option for everything from baking to seasoning meats.

Final Thoughts

Incorporating these spices into our daily meals doesn't have to be complicated. Start small by adding a pinch of these spices to your favorite recipes and gradually increase their presence in your diet. I like to start my day with a cup of ginger tea, and I assure you that once you sprinkle a little turmeric on your scrambled eggs, you'll never look back!

When it comes to adding herbs and spices to your diet, variety is crucial. The diverse array of bioactive compounds found in different herbs and spices work best synergistically, providing a broad spectrum of benefits beyond what any single spice could deliver alone. By experimenting with various combinations of spices, we can not only enrich our diets with a range of nutrients but also keep meals exciting and full of flavor.

Many herbs and spices are also rich in antioxidants, which is a lovely bonus! Just remember that herbs and spices work best as part of an overall healthy eating pattern. Accompanying these spices with plenty of fruits, vegetables, lean proteins, and whole grains will provide the most substantial health benefits. Sprinkling cinnamon on our takeaway might *technically* be adding to its nutritional value, but the takeaway is still far from being good for us!

Problem Foods and Their Properties

The fact is that processed foods have a significant impact on inflammation within our bodies. These convenience-based items, often lauded for their long shelf life and ease of preparation, are filled with additives and preservatives designed to enhance flavor and maintain freshness. However, many of these substances provoke unwanted inflammatory responses. For instance, certain preservatives can trigger an immune response, leading to inflammation as the body attempts to fend off what it perceives as threats. The artificial colors and flavors often found in processed foods may contribute to allergic reactions and inflammation, affecting people differently depending on their sensitivities (LeWine, 2024).

Let's explore some recurring nutritional themes that such foods offer and why they are problematic.

Refined Sugars

When consumed, these sugars rapidly increase blood sugar levels. This sudden spike leads to the production of advanced glycation end-products (AGEs), compounds that emerge when sugar molecules attach to proteins or fats. AGEs can damage collagen and elastin fibers, accelerating the aging process while also provoking inflammatory responses. Chronic consumption of high-sugar diets has been associated with insulin resistance, a condition that further fuels inflammation and increases the risk of metabolic diseases. Instead of refined sugars, opting for natural sweeteners like honey or maple syrup in moderation can help control inflammation levels.

Trans Fats

Trans fats, commonly found in hydrogenated oils used extensively in baked goods, fast food, and margarine, are another dietary element known to exacerbate inflammation. Studies have shown that these fats not only increase levels of inflammatory markers in the bloodstream but also contribute to cardiovascular diseases (Juul et al., 2021). Trans fats alter cell membrane structures, disrupting normal cellular functions and promoting chronic inflammation. There is also evidence suggesting they raise low-density lipoprotein (LDL) cholesterol, often termed 'bad' cholesterol, which clogs arteries and raises the risk of heart disease (Juul et al., 2021). Many countries have taken steps to ban or restrict trans fats due to their harmful health effects, highlighting the necessity for individuals to scrutinize ingredient labels and steer clear of foods containing partially hydrogenated oils.

Ultra-Processed Foods

The rise of ultra-processed foods deserves special attention. High in calories but low in nutritional value, these foods not only replace healthier options like fruits and vegetables but also lead to deficiencies in essential nutrients known to counteract inflammation. Ultra-processed foods often contain a high omega-6 to omega-3 ratio, creating an imbalance that promotes inflammation. While omega-6 fatty acids are essential fats needed for brain function and normal growth, excessive intake can tilt the balance toward inflammation.

Artificial Sweeteners

Artificial sweeteners and emulsifiers found in many diet sodas and packaged foods are also under scrutiny for their potential role in inflammation. Though low in calories, artificial sweeteners like aspartame and sucralose can disrupt gut microbiota, which plays a critical role in maintaining immune function and reducing inflammation. Emulsifiers, used to extend shelf life and improve texture, have been suggested in animal studies to increase the pro-inflammatory potential of the gut microbiome. Limiting consumption of these ingredients may reduce inflammation risks for those of us sensitive to gut bacteria changes (Juul et al., 2021).

A Lack of Fibrous Cell Walls

Did you know that the physical structure of food also has implications for inflammation? Processed foods tend to lack the fibrous cell walls needed to naturally slow nutrient absorption and promote healthy digestion. In contrast, the acellular structure of many ultra-processed foods allows rapid nutrient release, overwhelming digestive processes and potentially fostering an inflammatory gut environment (Juul et al., 2021). Whole, minimally processed foods help maintain a balanced gut microbiome, thereby supporting immune function and reducing inflammation markers. Simple switches, like choosing whole grains over refined counterparts, can make a considerable difference.

Impact on Energy and Pain Relief

So, what's the sum of everything we've covered in this chapter? What does it all mean, and how and why can anti-inflammatory foods boost our energy levels and alleviate pain?

The secret lies in how these foods interact with our cellular health. When we consume anti-inflammatory foods, our bodies are better equipped to fight off the oxidative stress and free radical damage that often leads to chronic inflammation. As a result, the cells operate more efficiently, leading to improved energy levels and reduced fatigue.

Boosting Energy Levels

Consuming a diet rich in antioxidants and essential nutrients found in fruits, vegetables, and fatty fish can greatly enhance our body's ability to produce energy. These foods are not only nourishing but also support the mitochondria—the powerhouse of cells—resulting in enhanced energy production. Consuming omega-3 fatty acids from sources like salmon or flaxseeds helps reduce inflammation and improve cellular function. This reduction in inflammation can directly translate to feeling more awake and energized throughout the day.

Including berries such as blueberries and blackberries in your diet also introduces anthocyanins, powerful antioxidants known for their anti-inflammatory properties. These compounds boost immune function and contribute to stable energy levels, preventing the typical afternoon slump. Ensuring an adequate intake of vitamins and minerals from diverse, colorful fruits and vegetables supports sustained energy release rather than sudden spikes and crashes.

Alleviating Pain

In parallel to energy enhancement, anti-inflammatory foods also play a crucial role in alleviating pain, especially joint pain that plagues many due to conditions like arthritis. Foods like turmeric, ginger, and leafy greens offer significant relief through their natural pain-relieving qualities. Turmeric contains curcumin, a compound that has been shown to be as effective as some over-the-counter pain medications, without adverse side effects. Studies indicate that regular consumption of curcumin can hinder the production of inflammatory molecules like cytokines and enzymes, reducing pain and swelling (Hobbs, 2024).

Similarly, ginger acts as a natural remedy, thanks to its active compounds, gingerols, which have both anti-inflammatory and antioxidant effects. I personally found an increase in both my mobility and flexibility once I consistently enjoyed ginger in my tea and turmeric in my weekly curries!

Foods That Do Both

The above benefits are great, but what's even better and more beneficial are the ingredients that can provide both health benefits simultaneously.

Whole grains and healthy fats, like those found in avocados and nuts, not only maintain energy levels by preventing blood sugar fluctuations but also supply essential fatty acids and fiber that further combat inflammation. Healthy fats help lubricate joints and keep tendons supple, contributing to smoother movements and increased physical capability.

Greater Mental Clarity

The overall vitality fostered by consuming anti-inflammatory foods extends beyond mere physical benefits. When our bodies are free from the burden of constant inflammation, mental clarity and performance are significantly enhanced. Mental fatigue, often exacerbated by poor dietary choices, can be mitigated by consuming foods that support brain health. Omega-3 fatty acids found in fatty fish like mackerel or sardines are particularly beneficial for cognitive function, promoting sharper focus and faster processing speeds.

By reducing systemic inflammation, including inflammation affecting the brain, we can enjoy not only clearer thinking but also improved and more stabilized moods. This holistic approach to diet ensures that our bodies and minds function at their best, supporting overall productivity and well-being.

Concluding Thoughts

Throughout this chapter, we've taken a deep dive into how anti-inflammatory foods work their magic to boost our health and keep inflammation-related diseases at bay. We've covered some of the superstars in an anti-inflammatory diet, such as leafy greens, berries, fatty fish, whole grains, nuts, seeds, and even spices like turmeric and ginger. Each has its unique way of fighting inflammation, providing essential nutrients to suppress inflammatory processes at the cellular level.

In essence, anti-inflammatory foods present a natural, accessible avenue toward better health. With their robust ability to enhance energy, alleviate pain, and promote vitality, they serve as potent allies in a wellness-focused lifestyle. Transitioning to a diet rich in anti-inflammatory foods requires mindfulness and dedication, but the positive outcomes on one's energy, mobility, and mental clarity make it a rewarding journey. Integrating these foods into everyday meals doesn't necessitate drastic changes but rather a conscious choice toward healthier alternatives.

Before we conclude, remember the following steps for the long-term reduction of inflammation:

1. Consider reducing your intake of processed foods laden with additives and preservatives.
2. Seek out fresh, whole foods that provide essential nutrients without triggering inflammatory responses.
3. Read nutrition labels carefully to identify hidden sugars and trans fats.
4. Opt for cooking at home using fresh ingredients, allowing you to control what goes into your meals.
5. Minimize sources of added sugars, favoring naturally occurring sugars in fruits instead.

Our next chapter will jump right into some delicious anti-inflammatory meals.

Chapter 2:

Exploring the Health Benefits of Delicious Anti-Inflammatory Meals

Exploring anti-inflammatory meals is a culinary adventure that brings health benefits to your table. This chapter dives into the significance of embracing an anti-inflammatory diet, shedding light on how this dietary shift can enhance overall wellness and vitality. It's a journey of flavors and textures that not only tantalizes the taste buds but also promotes long-term health improvements. By focusing on foods rich in antioxidants and healthy fats, you'll discover the profound impact that mindful eating can have on reducing inflammation, boosting immune function, and improving mood and energy levels.

In this chapter, I'll guide you through meal inspiration for every time of day, starting with scrumptious breakfast ideas that lay a healthy foundation for your mornings. From savory omelets bursting with vegetables to overnight oats infused with nature's sweetness, these meals are crafted to nourish your body from within. As we progress, enticing lunch selections and delectable dinner options take center stage, each thoughtfully composed to support your anti-inflammatory goals. We'll delve into snacks that satisfy cravings without compromising your commitment to health, presenting wholesome choices that fit seamlessly into your daily routine. To top it off, our delightful dessert suggestions prove that treats can be both delicious and nutritious, ensuring a balanced approach to enjoying sweet indulgences. Throughout, you'll gain insights into ingredient selection and preparation techniques that empower you to create meals bursting with flavor and vitality.

The recipes for every delicious meal that we cover in this chapter will be provided in the chapters that follow. As well as a few bonus smoothie and drink recipes!

Breakfast

Embarking on an anti-inflammatory diet can seem daunting, but breakfast offers a delicious opportunity to start your day with foods that fuel and foster well-being. Infusing your morning routine with meals focused on reducing inflammation can set a positive tone for the rest of the day. By incorporating ingredients rich in antioxidants, healthy fats, vitamins, and minerals, you're investing in long-term health benefits. Let's dive into some enticing breakfast options designed to reduce inflammation.

Spinach and Mushroom Omelet

The spinach and mushroom omelet is a classic option that never fails to impress with its nutrient density. Spinach, known for its high levels of vitamins A, C, and K, works wonders in fighting inflammation. It also contains iron and magnesium, essential minerals that play key roles in maintaining bodily function. Coupled with mushrooms, which boast selenium, copper, and B vitamins, this omelet is a powerhouse of anti-inflammatory goodness. Mushrooms also contain phenols and other antioxidants that provide protective effects against inflammation (Wartenberg & Spritzler, 2023).

Blueberry Almond Overnight Oats

First up, Blueberry Almond Overnight Oats provide a perfect combination of taste and nutrition. These oats are soaked overnight in almond milk, allowing them to absorb nutrients more effectively. Packed with antioxidants, blueberries not only add a burst of flavor but also work diligently to combat oxidative stress and inflammation in the body. Almonds, on the other hand, offer a generous dose of healthy fats, which aid in reducing inflammation markers.

Avocado Toast With Turmeric Eggs

Next on our list is Avocado Toast With Turmeric Eggs, a modern twist on a beloved classic. Avocado is celebrated for its healthy monounsaturated fats and antioxidant carotenoids, both of which contribute to reducing inflammation (Wartenberg & Spritzler, 2023). Adding eggs seasoned with turmeric elevates this meal's anti-inflammatory properties even further. Turmeric contains curcumin, an active compound known for its ability to inhibit pro-inflammatory molecules.

Chia Seed Pudding With Mixed Berries

For those with a sweet tooth, Chia Seed Pudding With Mixed Berries offers a delightful option brimming with nutritional advantages. Chia seeds are tiny powerhouses packed with omega-3 fatty acids that help counteract inflammation by balancing excessive omega-6 fatty acids in most diets. Mixed berries like strawberries, raspberries, and blackberries contribute additional antioxidants, further enhancing this breakfast's ability to fight inflammation (Wartenberg & Spritzler, 2023).

Anti-Inflammatory Breakfast Smoothie

An anti-inflammatory breakfast smoothie, packed with spinach, banana, ginger, pineapple, and flax or chia seeds, can provide a wealth of antioxidants, which help combat oxidative stress and inflammation in the body. Fresh ginger also aids digestion and can reduce gastrointestinal discomfort. Meanwhile, the flax or chia seeds supply omega-3 fatty acids and fiber, promoting heart health and digestive regularity.

The smoothie is naturally sweet, thanks to the banana and pineapple, which also provide essential vitamins and minerals, including potassium and vitamin C. The addition of unsweetened almond milk adds creaminess while being low in calories, hydrating the body without the need for excessive sugar.

Incorporating these breakfast ideas into your anti-inflammatory meal plan ignites a chain reaction within your body. Not only do you begin to ward off chronic diseases linked to inflammation, such as heart disease and diabetes, but you also pave the way for increased energy and improved mood. Emphasizing natural ingredients rich in antioxidants, healthy fats, and vital nutrients sets a solid foundation for your wellness journey.

Lunchtime

Lunch is a pivotal meal in maintaining an anti-inflammatory diet, offering an opportunity to nourish the body with ingredients known for their health benefits. Let's explore some delectable lunch options that not only tantalize your taste buds but also help reduce inflammation.

Quinoa Salad With Avocado and Chickpeas

A fantastic choice to kick off your lunchtime journey is the Quinoa Salad With Avocado and Chickpeas. This salad serves as a powerhouse of plant-based proteins and fiber, making it both satisfying and nutritious. Quinoa is a complete protein, containing all nine essential amino acids, which makes it perfect for those looking to increase their protein intake without consuming meat. Additionally, it's gluten-free and easily digestible. The chickpeas bring additional protein and fiber to the dish, contributing to digestive health and promoting a feeling of fullness that can help prevent overeating. Avocado adds creaminess and healthy fats, particularly monounsaturated fats, which are known to help lower bad cholesterol levels in the blood, further supporting heart health. These elements combined result in a flavorful, nutrient-packed salad that aligns well with anti-inflammatory goals.

Mediterranean Lentil Soup

Moving on, another excellent choice is Mediterranean Lentil Soup. This hearty soup is renowned for its inclusion of herbs and spices with potent anti-inflammatory properties. Lentils themselves are rich in dietary fiber, protein, iron, and folate, which contribute to improved digestion and energy levels. What truly sets this soup apart, however, is the array of herbs and spices infused into it. Ingredients like garlic, cumin, and coriander each boast unique health benefits. For example, garlic has been shown to stimulate the immune system and help fight inflammation. The warmth and richness of this soup make it a comforting choice, perfect for warding off unwanted inflammation while enjoying a delicious meal.

Grilled Chicken Salad With Balsamic Dressing

For those who crave something a bit lighter yet equally nourishing, the Grilled Chicken Salad With Balsamic Dressing is a splendid option. This salad takes advantage of lean protein sources, namely chicken, which is essential for muscle repair and growth while being low in fat. Incorporating grilled chicken into your salad ensures you're getting necessary nutrients without excess calories or unhealthy fats. But this salad's benefits don't stop there; it's also enhanced by the addition of colorful vegetables, rich in phytonutrients. These compounds found in plants provide numerous health benefits, including fighting inflammation and promoting eye health. The balsamic dressing not only elevates the flavor profile with its tangy sweetness but also offers potential health benefits due to its antioxidant content. Combined, these elements create a balanced, tasty meal that helps manage inflammation while delighting the palate.

Tuna and Cucumber Lettuce Wraps

Tuna and Cucumber Lettuce Wraps present a refreshing and nutritious lunch alternative. Tuna is an exceptional source of omega-3 fatty acids, which are crucial in combating inflammation throughout the body. Consuming omega-3s regularly has been associated with a decreased risk of chronic diseases such as heart disease and arthritis. Additionally, cucumbers provide hydration due to their high water content, aiding in flushing out toxins and keeping the skin healthy. Using lettuce leaves as wraps instead of traditional bread or tortillas reduces calorie intake and increases the meal's nutrient density. Adding other ingredients like celery and red onion can provide extra crunch and nutrients, rounding out this simple yet effective anti-inflammatory meal.

Roasted Veggie Bowl With Lemon-Tahini Dressing

Roasted veggie bowls with a zingy lemon-tahini dressing are a fantastic lunch option. The variety of vegetables provide a wide range of essential vitamins, minerals, and antioxidants that support overall health and well-being. The vegetables and quinoa or brown rice (depending on your preference) also contribute to a high fiber content, promoting digestive health and helping to maintain a healthy weight.

The olive oil and tahini are sources of healthy fats, which are important for heart health and can help reduce inflammation in the body. Furthermore, quinoa and tahini are plant-based proteins, making this meal suitable for vegetarians and vegans.

The dish is low in calories, meaning it can help with weight management while providing satisfaction and fullness, all while the vegetables help to keep us hydrated!

Dinner

Baked Salmon With Sweet Potatoes and Asparagus

Baked Salmon With Sweet Potatoes and Asparagus is a delightful recipe that harmoniously blends flavors while packing a powerful nutritional punch. The salmon, rich in omega-3 fatty acids, plays a pivotal role in reducing inflammation and promoting heart health. Omega-3s are essential fats your body can't produce on its own, found abundantly in fatty fish like salmon.

Sweet potatoes contribute to this dish by offering a good source of beta-carotene, an antioxidant that the body converts into vitamin A. This nutrient is vital for maintaining healthy skin and vision while supporting the immune system's function. Sweet potatoes are also high in fiber, which aids in digestion and helps maintain a healthy gut microbiome.

Asparagus rounds out the meal as another antioxidant-rich component, providing vitamins E, C, and K. It also contains important minerals like folate and chromium, which assist in transporting blood sugar from the bloodstream into cells, helping regulate inflammation. When baked alongside sweet potatoes and salmon, asparagus adds a pleasant crunch and a complementary flavor profile to the meal.

Turmeric Chicken Stir-Fry With Veggies

Another delectable anti-inflammatory dinner choice is Turmeric Chicken Stir-Fry With Veggies. Turmeric is renowned as a potent anti-inflammatory spice and has been used for centuries in traditional medicine. Its active compound, curcumin, offers numerous health benefits, including reducing inflammation markers throughout the body.

In this recipe, chicken serves as a lean protein source that fuels muscle growth and repair. Combining it with a variety of colorful vegetables, such as bell peppers, broccoli, and snap peas, amplifies the stir-fry's nutritional value. Each vegetable contributes a unique array of vitamins, minerals, and antioxidants. For instance, bell peppers are bursting with vitamin C, bolstering the immune system, while broccoli provides vitamin K and potent compounds like sulforaphane, known for their anti-inflammatory effects.

To create an even richer taste, stir-frying these ingredients in a splash of olive or coconut oil enhances flavor while supplying healthy fats that further help reduce inflammation levels. Adding ginger and garlic can elevate the aroma and taste, contributing additional anti-inflammatory benefits.

Lentil Curry With Spinach

Lentil Curry With Spinach offers a warm, comforting dish that nourishes the body while soothing inflammatory pathways. Lentils are little powerhouses of nutrition, packed with plant-based proteins and fibers that support digestive health. They also supply minerals like magnesium and iron, which are essential for cellular functions and energy production.

Spinach, a leafy green often dubbed a "superfood," plays a crucial role in combating inflammation. It's loaded with vitamins A, C, and K; magnesium; and various antioxidants, all serving to safeguard the body against oxidative stress. Adding spinach to lentil curry not only boosts its nutritional content but also introduces a velvety texture and earthy undertones.

The spices typically used in the curry—such as cumin and turmeric—work synergistically to enhance the dish's anti-inflammatory properties.

Baked Spinach and Feta Pasta

Baked Spinach and Feta Pasta is a delightfully creamy and filling dish that offers a wealth of health benefits. Spinach is packed with vitamins A, C, and K, as well as magnesium and iron, which are essential for overall health. Additionally, the high dietary fiber content, owing to a combination of pasta and spinach, aids in digestion and helps maintain a healthy gut.

The feta cheese and pasta contribute to the protein content of the dish, which is important for muscle repair and growth. Moreover, olive oil is a source of healthy monounsaturated fats, which can support heart health and reduce inflammation.

This particular dish is low in calories, and high in antioxidants thanks to the tomatoes and spinach, while the combination of spinach and dairy provides calcium and other nutrients that promote strong bones.

Zucchini Noodles With Pesto and Grilled Shrimp

Zucchini Noodles With Pesto and Grilled Shrimp is a vibrant, light dinner dish that is refreshingly low in calories, making it a great option for maintaining a healthy weight. The meal includes fresh basil, zucchini, and shrimp, which provide essential vitamins, minerals, and antioxidants that contribute to overall health. Plus, it is high in protein, with 23 grams of protein per serving from the grilled shrimp, supporting muscle growth and repair, making it great for active individuals.

The olive oil used in both the pesto and the shrimp contributes heart-healthy monounsaturated fats, which can help improve cholesterol levels. At the same time, the zucchini is high in fiber, which aids digestion, helps maintain healthy blood sugar levels, and promotes a feeling of fullness.

The blend of carbohydrates, protein, and fats creates a balanced meal that can provide sustained energy and prevent spikes in blood sugar, while the basil, garlic, and olive oil have anti-inflammatory and antioxidant properties, which can help protect the body from chronic diseases.

Snacks and Sides

With the right ingredients, your snacks can contribute effectively to your health goals. Here are some delightful choices to consider:

Turmeric Roasted Chickpeas

One of the best snacks you can have on hand is Turmeric Roasted Chickpeas. These crunchy, nutrient-dense bites are not only satisfying but also pack a punch when it comes to anti-inflammatory benefits. Chickpeas, also known as garbanzo beans, are high in fiber and protein, which help keep you full longer, preventing unhealthy snacking urges. More importantly, when roasted with turmeric, they become even more beneficial for reducing inflammation. Turmeric contains curcumin, a compound known for its powerful antioxidant and anti-inflammatory properties. To enhance the absorption of curcumin, pair turmeric with black pepper or a healthy fat source. Turmeric Roasted Chickpeas can be enjoyed on their own or sprinkled atop salads for added texture and flavor.

Avocado Hummus With Carrot Sticks

For those who enjoy creamy and rich snacks, Avocado Hummus With Carrot Sticks is an excellent choice. The avocado provides a good dose of healthy fats, specifically monounsaturated fats, which are known to reduce bad cholesterol levels and decrease inflammation. By combining avocados with chickpeas to make hummus, you get a double hit of nutritious benefits while keeping it delicious. Carrot sticks add crunch and serve as a great vessel for the creamy dip. They're rich in vitamins, particularly beta-carotene, which has been linked to anti-inflammatory effects. Such a snack not only satiates hunger but also nourishes the body with impactful compounds.

Spinach and Mushroom Mini Frittatas

The combination of spinach, mushroom, and egg in these gorgeous little frittatas creates a powerful nutritional boost.

Spinach has beneficial nutrients such as vitamins A, C, and K. These vitamins help maintain healthy vision, support the immune system, and play a crucial role in skin health by promoting collagen production and fighting free radicals. Additionally, they are important for blood clotting and bone health.

Mushrooms have heart-protecting properties, are low in calories, and provide a good amount of antioxidants, which help protect the body from damage caused by harmful molecules known as free radicals.

And then there's the hearty protein boost from the eggs, and an extra boost of bone strengthening calcium from milk and cheese, wrapping up the incredible array of nutritional benefits offered by this quick and easy snack!

Peanut Butter Energy Balls

These compact snacks provide a quick and sustained energy boost, making them perfect for busy individuals or those needing a pre- or post-workout nibble. The primary ingredient, peanut butter, is packed with protein and healthy fats, both of which contribute to long-lasting energy levels. Proteins serve as building blocks for muscles, tissues, and cells, supporting muscle repair and growth, which is essential for anyone involved in physical activities.

What makes these energy balls particularly effective for satiety and digestive health is the incorporation of oats. Oats are high in dietary fiber, particularly beta-glucan, which contributes to better digestion and helps maintain a feeling of fullness long after consumption. This quality is invaluable for those looking to manage weight or avoid unhealthy snacking between meals. By keeping you satiated, fiber-rich foods like oats stabilize blood sugar levels and prevent energy crashes, common when consuming simple carbohydrates.

For people who enjoy versatility, these energy balls allow for creativity in ingredients while maintaining their nutritional value. One might consider substitutes like almond or cashew butter if peanut butter is not available or preferred. Additional elements such as flaxseeds further enhance the omega-3 fatty acid content, contributing to heart health and reducing inflammation in the body.

Dark Chocolate Trail Mix

Dark Chocolate Trail Mix is a delicious blend that harnesses the natural health benefits of its ingredients, bringing antioxidant properties to the forefront. Dark chocolate itself is rich in flavonoids, which are powerful antioxidants that help combat oxidative stress. Oxidative stress occurs when there are too many free radicals in the body, potentially leading to chronic diseases such as heart disease and cancer. By neutralizing these harmful molecules, dark chocolate supports overall cellular health and protects against damage. Nuts and seeds included in the trail mix further enhance its health benefits. They contain omega-3 fatty acids, which are essential for promoting heart health. Omega-3s work by reducing inflammation in the body, lowering blood pressure, and improving the balance between HDL (good) cholesterol and LDL (bad) cholesterol levels. This helps reduce the risk of cardiovascular diseases, making dark chocolate trail mix not only a tasty snack but also a heart-healthy choice.

In addition, nuts and seeds add more antioxidants to the mix. For example, almonds and walnuts are high in vitamin E, another antioxidant that helps protect skin from oxidative damage and maintains healthy hair and eyes. Pumpkin seeds contain zinc and magnesium, which support immune function and improve sleep quality. Incorporating this trail mix into your diet not only satisfies cravings but also provides a host of nutrients beneficial for overall well-being.

Desserts

Enticing desserts can be part of a balanced anti-inflammatory diet, providing delightful options that support your health journey. A suitable dessert not only satisfies sweet cravings but also contributes to reducing inflammation in the body. With mindful ingredient selections, you can create mouthwatering treats that nourish rather than hinder your health.

Avocado Brownies

Avocado Brownies are a delightful and nutritious twist on the classic dessert, offering a myriad of health benefits due to their wholesome ingredients. Often associated with unhealthy indulgence, these calorie-conscious brownies present a unique opportunity to satisfy your sweet tooth while prioritizing your well-being. One key ingredient that elevates these treats is the avocado, a fruit celebrated for its rich content of healthy monounsaturated fats. Unlike saturated fats found in butter or traditional baking oils, monounsaturated fats can support heart health by reducing levels of bad cholesterol (LDL) while maintaining or even increasing good cholesterol (HDL). This balance is crucial for cardiovascular wellness and can effectively lower the risk of heart disease.

Incorporating avocados into your desserts not only contributes to heart health but also aids digestion. Avocados are an excellent source of dietary fiber, essential for a healthy digestive system. Fiber helps regulate bowel movements, prevents constipation, and promotes the feeling of fullness after eating. This can be particularly beneficial if you're watching your weight. The satiating power of fiber can curb unnecessary snacking and overeating, making avocado brownies a smart choice for those aiming to manage their caloric intake without sacrificing flavor.

Beyond fats and fiber, avocados are packed with vital vitamins such as K, E, C, and B-6, each contributing uniquely to maintaining overall health. Vitamin K plays a crucial role in blood clotting and bone health, while vitamin E acts as a potent antioxidant, protecting cells from oxidative damage. Vitamin C is renowned for its immune-boosting properties, helping the body fend off infections and illnesses, while vitamin B-6 supports brain health and energy metabolism. Consuming foods rich in these vitamins ensures a robust immune system and keeps various physiological processes functioning optimally.

Almond Flour Pancakes With Berries

Almond Flour Pancakes With Berries are a delightful and nutritious twist on traditional dessert choices, offering not just great taste but also impressive health benefits. For those seeking sustained energy throughout the day, this combination can be an excellent option. Let's delve deeper into how these ingredients contribute to long-lasting vitality and stable energy levels.

One of the standout features of almond flour is its protein content. Protein is essential for building and repairing tissues, but it also plays an important role in maintaining energy levels. Proteins are broken down into amino acids, which serve as building blocks for many of the body's processes, including metabolism. This slow digestion of proteins helps you feel fuller for longer periods, thereby reducing the need for mid-morning snack binges that send blood sugar levels spiraling.

Healthy fats also play a crucial part in sustaining energy. Almond flour is rich in monounsaturated fats, particularly oleic acid, which is known to support heart health and reduce inflammation. These fats are digested gradually, helping to maintain steady energy levels. Additionally, healthy fats support cellular function by providing essential fatty acids necessary for optimal brain activity and overall well-being.

Complementing the almond flour, berries bring their own unique set of nutrients to this energizing breakfast. Berries such as blueberries, strawberries, and raspberries are packed full of antioxidants. These powerful compounds are crucial in fighting oxidative stress and reducing inflammation, which can otherwise lead to fatigue and decreased vitality. Antioxidants neutralize free radicals—unstable molecules that can cause damage to cells—and thus play a protective role in enhancing overall health.

Lemon Blueberry Cheesecake Bars

Lemon Blueberry Cheesecake Bars are not only delicious but also bring several health benefits that can contribute positively to your overall well-being. One of the key components of these bars is blueberries. These small, vibrant fruits are loaded with antioxidants, which play a crucial role in keeping our bodies healthy. Antioxidants help fight against oxidative stress, which is caused by free radicals in the body. By consuming foods rich in antioxidants, such as blueberries, you may lower the risk of developing chronic diseases, including heart disease, diabetes, and even some cancers. So, when you enjoy a Lemon Blueberry Cheesecake Bar, you are treating your taste buds and supporting your health simultaneously.

Another important ingredient in these bars is lemon. Lemons are not only known for their tart flavor but are also an excellent source of vitamin C, which is essential for a variety of bodily functions. It supports the immune system, helping to fend off illnesses. Vitamin C is also beneficial for skin health, as it aids in collagen production, necessary for maintaining skin elasticity and reducing wrinkles. Furthermore, vitamin C enhances the absorption of iron from plant-based foods. Since iron is vital for producing healthy red blood cells, incorporating lemon into your diet can help improve your overall health. When you enjoy a Lemon Blueberry Cheesecake Bar, you are getting a tasty dose of vitamin C that your body needs.

Lastly, enjoying Lemon Blueberry Cheesecake Bars can also be a great way to boost your mood. The combination of lemon and blueberry flavors can create a delightful experience. Food has a powerful connection to our mood and emotions. Sweet treats, when eaten in moderation, can provide a sense of satisfaction and happiness. The flavors from the lemon and blueberries can uplift your spirits, making these bars not just a treat for your taste buds but also a way to improve your mood. Savoring a piece of lemon blueberry cheesecake after a long day can act as a small reward, contributing to feelings of comfort and joy.

Sweet Potato Pie

Sweet Potato Pie offers several health benefits, including being a good source of vitamins A and C, which support immune function and skin health. It also contains fiber, aiding digestion and promoting a feeling of fullness. Additionally, sweet potatoes have antioxidants that may help reduce inflammation and protect against chronic diseases. Sweet Potato Pie can be a healthier dessert option compared to other pies, especially when made with natural sweeteners and whole ingredients!

Tart Cherry Nice Cream

Tart Cherry Nice Cream, made predominantly from tart cherries, offers several health benefits. Firstly, tart cherries are high in antioxidants, which help combat oxidative stress and reduce inflammation in the body. Furthermore, the anthocyanins found in tart cherries may help further reduce muscle soreness and inflammation, making it beneficial for athletes and active individuals. Tart cherries also contain natural melatonin, which can help regulate sleep patterns and improve overall sleep quality while potentially contributing to heart health by improving cholesterol levels and reducing the risk of heart disease. As a low-calorie dessert option, Tart Cherry Nice Cream can also satisfy sweet cravings while helping with weight management, supporting our immune system thanks to its high vitamin and antioxidant content. Lastly, the fiber found in tart cherries aids digestion and helps maintain a healthy gut.

Concluding Thoughts

Incorporating these meals into our lives involves more than just swapping ingredients; it's about embracing foods that provide health benefits while indulging our taste buds. Now all that's left to do is learn how to make them all. We're starting with breakfast!

Chapter 3:

Quick, Easy, Anti-Inflammatory Breakfasts

Spinach and Mushroom Omelet

Wellness Wonders: Benefits

This flavorful omelet combines antioxidant-rich spinach and mushrooms, creating a protein-packed, anti-inflammatory meal that supports immune health and provides lasting energy.

Yield: 1 serving

Prep: 5 minutes

Cook: 7–11 minutes

Total Time: 12–16 minutes

Nutritional Information:

Cals	Carbs	Fat	Protein	Fiber
280	7g	22g	18g	2g

Ingredients:

- 1 tbsp olive oil or butter
- 1/2 cup mushrooms, sliced
- 1/2 cup fresh spinach, chopped
- 2 large eggs, beaten
- salt and pepper (to taste)
- optional: A sprinkle of cheese (e.g., feta or cheddar)

Instructions:

1. In a non-stick skillet, add 1 tablespoon of olive oil or butter.
2. Heat the skillet over medium heat for about 1 minute until the oil is hot but not smoking.
3. Sauté the mushrooms for about 3–4 minutes, stirring occasionally, until they are soft and slightly golden in color.
4. Once the mushrooms are cooked, add the chopped spinach to the skillet. Sauté for an additional 1–2 minutes until the spinach is wilted.
5. Season the eggs with the salt and pepper (if desired), then pour them over the sautéed mushrooms and spinach in the skillet.
6. Gently lift the edges of the omelet with a spatula, tilting the skillet to allow the uncooked eggs to flow to the edges. Cook for about 2–3 minutes until the eggs are set but still slightly moist on top.
7. If using cheese, sprinkle it on one half of the omelet.
8. Carefully fold the omelet in half using a spatula.
9. Cook for an additional 1–2 minutes, or until the cheese (if added) is melted, and the eggs are fully cooked.
10. Slide the omelet onto a plate and serve hot.

Blueberry Almond Overnight Oats

Wellness Wonders: Benefits

This wholesome breakfast combines antioxidant-rich blueberries with fiber-packed oats and vitamin E from almonds, delivering a satisfying, anti-inflammatory meal that supports heart health and boosts immunity.

Yield: 2 servings

Prep: 10 minutes

Chill: 4 hours+

Cook: N/A

Total Time: 4 hours 10 minutes+

Nutritional Information:

Cals	Carbs	Fat	Protein	Fiber
350	50g	12g	14g	8g

Ingredients:

- 1 cup rolled oats
- 1 1/2 cups almond milk (or other milk of choice)
- 1/2 cup Greek yogurt (or plant-based yogurt)
- 1 tbsp honey or maple syrup (optional for sweetness)
- 1/2 tsp vanilla extract
- 1/4 tsp cinnamon
- 1 cup fresh blueberries (or frozen)
- 2 tbsp almond butter
- 1/4 cup sliced almonds (for topping)

Instructions:

1. In a medium bowl, combine the rolled oats, almond milk, Greek yogurt, honey (or maple syrup), vanilla extract, almond butter, and cinnamon. Stir well until all ingredients are fully mixed.
2. Gently fold in the blueberries, making sure they are evenly distributed throughout the mixture.
3. Divide the oat mixture evenly into two airtight containers or jars. Seal them tightly.
4. Place the containers in the refrigerator and let the oats soak overnight (or at least for 4 hours) to allow the flavors to meld and the oats to absorb the liquid.
5. In the morning, take the containers out of the refrigerator. Stir the mixture if needed and top with sliced almonds before serving. You can also add a few more fresh blueberries on top for garnish.

Avocado Toast With Turmeric Eggs

Wellness Wonders: Benefits

This nourishing toast combines creamy avocado with anti-inflammatory turmeric-spiced eggs, creating a delicious, heart-healthy meal that supports brain function and immune health.

Yield: 2 servings

Prep: 10 minutes

Cook: 10 minutes

Total Time: 20 minutes

Nutritional Information:

Cals	Carbs	Fat	Protein	Fiber
360	34g	20g	12g	10g

Ingredients:

- 2 ripe avocados
- salt and pepper (to taste)
- 4 large eggs
- 1 tsp turmeric powder
- 4 slices of whole grain bread
- Optional toppings: cherry tomatoes, red pepper flakes, fresh herbs (e.g., cilantro, parsley)

Instructions:

1. Cut the ripe avocados in half, remove the pit, and scoop the flesh into a bowl.
2. Mash the avocado with a fork until creamy. Season with salt, pepper, and a squeeze of lemon juice, if desired.
3. In a skillet over medium heat, add a bit of olive oil or cooking spray.
4. Crack the eggs into the skillet and sprinkle the turmeric powder over them.
5. Scramble the eggs by stirring gently until cooked through.
6. Toast the whole grain bread slices in a toaster until golden brown and crispy.
7. Spread a generous amount of the mashed avocado on each slice of toasted bread.
8. Top each slice with a heap of the scrambled turmeric eggs.
9. Garnish the toast with cherry tomatoes, fresh herbs, or red pepper flakes for added flavor and presentation if desired.
10. Enjoy your avocado toast with turmeric eggs while it's warm!

Chia Seed Pudding With Mixed Berries

Wellness Wonders: Benefits

This creamy, fiber-rich pudding combines omega-3-packed chia seeds with antioxidant-loaded mixed berries, creating a satisfying, anti-inflammatory treat that supports heart health and immune function.

Yield: 4 servings

Prep: 10 minutes

Cook: N/A

Chill: 2 hours+

Total Time: 2 hours 10 minutes+

Nutritional Information:

Cals	Carbs	Fat	Protein	Fiber
150	19g	7g	5g	10g

Ingredients:

- 1/2 cup chia seeds
- 2 cups almond milk
- 2 tbsp maple syrup (or honey)
- 1 tsp vanilla extract
- 2 cups mixed berries (fresh or frozen, e.g., strawberries, blueberries, raspberries)
- optional toppings: nuts, coconut flakes, or additional fruits

Instructions:

1. In a medium bowl, whisk together the chia seeds, almond milk, maple syrup, and vanilla extract until well combined.
2. Let the mixture sit for about 5 minutes, then whisk again to prevent clumping of the chia seeds.
3. Cover the bowl with plastic wrap or transfer the mixture to individual serving cups or jars.
4. Refrigerate for at least 2 hours, or overnight, to allow the chia seeds to absorb the liquid and thicken.
5. If using fresh berries, wash and slice them as needed. If using frozen berries, allow them to thaw and drain any excess liquid.
6. Once the chia pudding has thickened, stir it gently to mix. Spoon it into bowls or cups.
7. Top each serving with a generous amount of mixed berries and any additional toppings like nuts or coconut flakes.
8. Serve the chia seed pudding chilled and enjoy as a nutritious breakfast!

Anti-Inflammatory Breakfast Smoothie

Wellness Wonders: Benefits

This nutrient-packed smoothie combines antioxidant-rich berries, anti-inflammatory turmeric, and omega-3-rich chia seeds, offering a refreshing drink that supports immune health and reduces inflammation.

Yield: 2 servings

Prep: 5 minutes

Cook: N/A

Total Time: 5 minutes

Nutritional Information:

Cals	Carbs	Fat	Protein	Fiber
180	36g	2g	4g	5g

Ingredients:

- 2 cups fresh spinach
- 1 ripe banana, peeled and sliced
- 1-inch fresh ginger, peeled and grated
- 1 cup unsweetened almond milk
- 1/2 cup pineapple chunks (fresh or frozen)
- 1 tbsp flaxseeds or chia seeds (optional)
- a dash of honey or maple syrup (optional)
- ice cubes (optional, for thickness)

Instructions:

1. Wash the fresh spinach thoroughly and remove any tough stems.
2. In a blender, add the spinach, banana, grated ginger, almond milk, and pineapple chunks.
3. If using flaxseeds or chia seeds, add them to the blender.
4. Add ice cubes if you prefer a thicker smoothie.
5. Blend the ingredients on high speed until smooth and creamy. If the mixture is too thick, you can add a little more almond milk to reach your desired consistency.
6. Taste the smoothie and adjust the sweetness if needed by adding a little honey or maple syrup, although the banana and pineapple should provide natural sweetness.
7. Serve in glasses immediately.
8. Garnish with a sprinkle of flax or chia seeds if desired.

Concluding Thoughts

Anti-inflammatory breakfasts are packed with all the nutritional power needed to see us coast through even the toughest mornings and prevent us from the midmorning lag! Next, we're going to look at a selection of energizing lunch recipes.

Chapter 4:

Energizing Lunch Recipes

Quinoa Salad With Avocado and Chickpeas

Wellness Wonders: Benefits

This refreshing salad combines protein-packed quinoa with creamy avocado and fiber-rich chickpeas, delivering a nutrient-dense, anti-inflammatory meal that supports heart health and promotes satiety.

Yield: 4 servings

Prep: 15 minutes

Cook: 15 minutes

Total Time: 30 minutes

Nutritional Information:

Cals	Carbs	Fat	Protein	Fiber
350	45g	15g	10g	10g

Ingredients:

- 1 cup quinoa
- 2 cups water
- 1 can (15 oz) chickpeas, drained and rinsed
- 1 ripe avocado, diced
- 1 cup cherry tomatoes, halved
- 1/2 cucumber, diced
- 1/4 red onion, finely chopped
- 1/4 cup fresh parsley, finely chopped
- 1/4 cup olive oil
- 2 tbsp lemon juice
- salt and pepper (to taste)

Instructions:

1. Rinse 1 cup of quinoa under cold water in a fine-mesh strainer.
2. In a medium saucepan, combine the rinsed quinoa and 2 cups of water.
3. Bring to a boil, then reduce heat to low, cover, and simmer for 15 minutes, or until the quinoa is tender and water is absorbed.
4. Remove from heat and let it sit covered for 5 minutes. Fluff with a fork and set aside to cool.
5. In a small bowl, whisk together the olive oil, lemon juice, salt, and pepper.

6. In a large bowl, combine the cooled quinoa, chickpeas, diced avocado, cherry tomatoes, cucumber, red onion, and parsley. Pour the dressing over the salad and toss gently to combine.

7. Taste and adjust seasoning, if necessary. Serve immediately or refrigerate for 30 minutes to allow flavors to meld. Enjoy!

Mediterranean Lentil Soup

Wellness Wonders: Benefits

This hearty, nourishing soup blends fiber-rich lentils with anti-inflammatory herbs, tomatoes, and greens, creating a meal that supports heart health, digestion, and immune function.

Yield: 6 servings

Prep: 15 minutes

Cook: 41–49 minutes

Total Time: 56 minutes – 1 hour 4 minutes

Nutritional Information:

Cals	Carbs	Fat	Protein	Fiber
200	35g	4g	12g	12g

Ingredients:

- 1 tbsp olive oil
- 1 onion, diced
- 2 carrots, diced
- 2 celery stalks, diced
- 3 garlic cloves, minced
- 1 tsp ground cumin
- 1 tsp ground coriander
- 1/2 tsp smoked paprika
- 1/4 tsp cayenne pepper
- 1 can (14 oz) diced tomatoes
- 1 cup dried lentils (green or brown), rinsed
- 6 cups vegetable broth
- 1 bay leaf
- 1 cup spinach or kale, chopped
- juice of 1 lemon
- salt and pepper (to taste)
- fresh parsley (for garnish)

Instructions:

1. In a large pot, heat the olive oil over medium heat. Add the diced onion, carrots, and celery. Sauté for about 5–7 minutes until the vegetables are softened.
2. Stir in the minced garlic, cumin, coriander, smoked paprika, and cayenne pepper. Cook for an additional 1–2 minutes until fragrant.

3. Add the diced tomatoes (with juices), rinsed lentils, and vegetable broth. Stir to combine and add the bay leaf. Bring to a boil.

4. Once boiling, reduce the heat to low, cover the pot, and let the soup simmer for about 30–35 minutes, or until the lentils are tender.

5. Stir in the chopped spinach or kale and lemon juice. Cook for another 5 minutes to soften the greens. Then remove the bay leaf.

6. Season the soup with salt and pepper to taste. Serve hot, garnished with fresh parsley.

Grilled Chicken Salad With Balsamic Dressing

Wellness Wonders: Benefits

This satisfying salad combines lean, protein-rich grilled chicken with antioxidant-packed greens and a tangy balsamic dressing, offering a heart-healthy, anti-inflammatory meal that supports immunity and overall wellness.

Yield: 4 servings

Prep: 10 minutes

Cook: 12–14 minutes

Total Time: 22–24 minutes

Nutritional Information:

Cals	Carbs	Fat	Protein	Fiber
290	15g	12g	30g	3g

Ingredients:

- 2 boneless, skinless chicken breasts
- 1 tbsp olive oil
- salt and pepper (to taste)
- 6 cups mixed greens (spinach, arugula, romaine)
- 1 cup cherry tomatoes, halved
- 1 cucumber, sliced
- 1/4 red onion, thinly sliced
- 1/4 cup feta cheese, crumbled (optional)
- 1/4 cup balsamic vinegar
- 1 tbsp honey
- 1 tsp Dijon mustard

Instructions:

1. Preheat the grill to medium-high heat. Brush the chicken breasts with olive oil and season with salt and pepper.
2. Place the chicken on the grill and cook for about 6–7 minutes on each side, or until the internal temperature reaches 165°F (75°C) and the chicken is no longer pink inside. Remove from the grill and let it rest for 5 minutes before slicing.
3. In a large bowl, combine the mixed greens, cherry tomatoes, cucumber, and red onion. If desired, add crumbled feta cheese.
4. In a small bowl, whisk together the balsamic vinegar, honey, and Dijon mustard. Drizzle in a little olive oil while whisking until well combined.
5. Slice the grilled chicken and add it to the salad mixture. Drizzle the balsamic dressing over the salad and toss gently to combine.
6. Divide the salad among four plates and serve immediately.

Tuna and Cucumber Lettuce Wraps

Wellness Wonders: Benefits

These light, refreshing wraps combine protein-rich tuna with hydrating cucumber in crisp lettuce, offering a nutrient-dense, anti-inflammatory meal that supports heart health and aids digestion.

Yield: 2 servings

Prep: 15 minutes

Cook: N/A

Total Time: 15 minutes

Nutritional Information:

Cals	Carbs	Fat	Protein	Fiber
220	8g	10g	27g	2g

Ingredients:

- 1 can (5 oz) tuna, drained
- 1/4 cup mayonnaise
- 1 tbsp Dijon mustard
- 1 tbsp lemon juice
- 1/4 cup celery, finely chopped
- 1/4 cup red onion, finely chopped
- salt and pepper (to taste)
- 1 large cucumber
- lettuce leaves (e.g., romaine or butter lettuce) for wrapping
- fresh herbs (e.g., dill or parsley) (optional garnish)

Instructions:

1. In a medium bowl, combine the drained tuna, mayonnaise, Dijon mustard, and lemon juice. Mix well.
2. Stir in the chopped celery and red onion. Season with salt and pepper to taste.
3. Cut the cucumber into thick slices to create "boats." Each slice will serve as a base for the tuna filling.
4. Rinse and dry the lettuce leaves. These will be used to wrap the cucumber slices if desired.
5. Place a cucumber slice on a lettuce leaf, then spoon a generous amount of the tuna mixture on top. If using, garnish with fresh herbs.
6. Roll the lettuce around the cucumber and tuna for a wrap effect or enjoy them open-faced. Serve immediately.

Roasted Veggie Bowl With Lemon-Tahini Dressing

Wellness Wonders: Benefits

This vibrant bowl combines a variety of roasted vegetables with a creamy lemon-tahini dressing, creating a fiber-rich, antioxidant-packed meal that reduces inflammation and supports digestive health.

Yield: 4 servings

Prep: 10 minutes

Cook: 30–35 minutes

Total Time: 40–45 minutes

Nutritional Information:

Cals	Carbs	Fat	Protein	Fiber
350	45g	15g	10g	8g

Ingredients:

- **Roasted Vegetables:**
  - 1 medium zucchini, diced
  - 1 bell pepper, diced
  - 1 medium carrot, sliced
  - 1 cup broccoli florets
  - 1 cup cauliflower florets
  - 2 tbsp olive oil
  - salt and pepper (to taste)
  - 1 tsp garlic powder
- **Lemon-Tahini Dressing:**
  - 1/4 cup tahini
  - 2 tbsp lemon juice
  - 1 tbsp olive oil
  - 1-2 tbsp warm water (to thin)
  - salt and pepper (to taste)
- **To Serve:**
  - 2 cups cooked quinoa or brown rice
  - fresh parsley or cilantro (optional garnish)

Ingredients:

1. Preheat the oven to 425°F (220°C).

2. In a large bowl, combine the diced zucchini, bell pepper, carrot, broccoli, and cauliflower. Drizzle with 2 tablespoons of olive oil, sprinkle with salt, pepper, and garlic powder. Toss to evenly coat the vegetables.
3. Spread the coated vegetables in a single layer on a baking sheet. Roast in the preheated oven for 20–25 minutes, or until the vegetables are tender and slightly caramelized, stirring halfway through.
4. While the vegetables are roasting, prepare the lemon-tahini dressing. In a small bowl, whisk together the tahini, lemon juice, olive oil, and enough warm water to achieve a smooth, pourable consistency. Season with salt and pepper to taste.
5. If not already cooked, prepare the quinoa or brown rice according to package instructions.
6. Once the vegetables are done roasting, remove them from the oven. In serving bowls, layer the cooked quinoa or brown rice, followed by the roasted vegetables.
7. Drizzle the lemon-tahini dressing over the top of each bowl. Garnish with fresh herbs if desired.
8. Enjoy your roasted veggie bowls warm!

Concluding Thoughts

These lunch recipes are packed with all of the dense nutrients you need to keep your energy levels high as your day reaches its midpoint. Next, we'll be making dinner!

Chapter 5:

Nourishing Dinner Recipes

Baked Salmon With Sweet Potatoes and Asparagus

Wellness Wonders: Benefits

This simple, one-pan meal combines omega-3-rich salmon with fiber-filled sweet potatoes and antioxidant-packed asparagus, creating a delicious dinner that supports heart health and reduces inflammation.

Yield: 4 servings

Prep: 10 minutes

Cook: 30–35 minutes

Total Time: 40–45 minutes

Nutritional Information:

Cals	Carbs	Fat	Protein	Fiber
400	35g	20g	30g	6g

Ingredients:

- 2 medium sweet potatoes, peeled and diced
- 3 tbsp olive oil
- 1 tsp garlic powder
- 1 tsp paprika
- 4 (6 oz) salmon fillets
- 1 bunch asparagus, trimmed
- 1 lemon, sliced (for garnish)
- fresh parsley (for garnish)
- salt and pepper (to taste)

Instructions:

1. Preheat the oven to 400°F (200°C).
2. On a baking sheet, toss the diced sweet potatoes with 1 tablespoon of olive oil, garlic powder, paprika, salt, and pepper. Spread in a single layer.
3. Bake the sweet potatoes in the preheated oven for 15 minutes.
4. While the sweet potatoes are baking, drizzle the salmon fillets with 1 tablespoon of olive oil and season with salt and pepper.
5. Place the salmon fillets on the baking sheet with the sweet potatoes after they've baked for 15 minutes.
6. Arrange the trimmed asparagus around the salmon and drizzle with the remaining 1 tablespoon of olive oil, seasoning with salt and pepper.

7. Return the baking sheet to the oven and bake everything for an additional 15–20 minutes, or until the salmon flakes easily with a fork and the sweet potatoes are tender.

8. Remove from the oven, garnish with lemon slices and fresh parsley, and serve hot.

Lentil Curry With Spinach

Wellness Wonders: Benefits

This hearty, flavorful curry combines fiber-rich lentils with anti-inflammatory spices and nutrient-dense spinach, providing a balanced meal that supports heart health.

Yield: 4 servings

Prep: 10 minutes

Cook: 30–40 minutes

Total Time: 40–50 minutes

Nutritional Information:

Cals	Carbs	Fat	Protein	Fiber
280	45g	5g	15g	12g

Ingredients:

- 1 tbsp olive oil
- 1 onion, diced
- 2 garlic cloves, minced
- 1 tbsp fresh ginger, grated
- 1 tbsp curry powder
- 1 tsp cumin
- 1 tsp turmeric
- 1 can (14 oz) diced tomatoes
- 1 cup dried lentils (red or green), rinsed
- 4 cups vegetable broth
- 2 cups fresh spinach, chopped
- salt and pepper (to taste)
- fresh cilantro (for garnish)
- 4 slices naan bread (for serving)

Instructions:

1. In a large pot, heat the olive oil over medium heat.
2. Add the diced onion and sauté for about 5–7 minutes until translucent. Stir in the minced garlic and grated ginger, cooking for an additional 1–2 minutes until fragrant.
3. Stir in the curry powder, cumin, and turmeric, cooking for another minute to toast the spices.
4. Add the diced tomatoes (with their juices) and rinsed lentils into the pot. Stir to combine.
5. Pour in the vegetable broth and bring the mixture to a boil. Reduce the heat to low, cover, and let it simmer for 20–25 minutes, or until the lentils are tender.

6. Once the lentils are cooked, stir in the chopped spinach and cook for an additional 3–5 minutes until the spinach wilts. Season with salt and pepper to taste.

7. Remove from heat and serve hot with naan bread. Garnish with fresh cilantro.

Turmeric Chicken Stir-Fry With Veggies

Wellness Wonders: Benefits

This vibrant stir-fry combines protein-packed chicken with anti-inflammatory turmeric and a mix of colorful vegetables, creating a nutrient-dense meal that supports immune health and reduces inflammation.

Yield: 4 servings

Prep: 15 minutes

Cook: 12–16 minutes

Total Time: 27–31 minutes

Nutritional Information:

Cals	Carbs	Fat	Protein	Fiber
350	30g	15g	30g	5g

Ingredients:

- 2 tbsp olive oil (or coconut oil)
- 1 pound (450g) boneless, skinless chicken breasts, sliced
- salt and pepper (to taste)
- 2 tbsp fresh turmeric root, grated
- 1 tbsp ginger, grated
- 3 garlic cloves, minced
- 2 cups bell peppers, sliced (red, yellow, and green)
- 1 cup broccoli florets
- 1 cup snap peas
- 2 tbsp soy sauce (or tamari for gluten-free)
- cooked rice or quinoa (for serving)
- fresh cilantro (for garnish)

Instructions:

1. In a large skillet or wok, heat the oil over medium-high heat.
2. Add the sliced chicken to the skillet. Season with salt and pepper. Cook for about 5–7 minutes, stirring occasionally, until the chicken is cooked through and no longer pink.
3. Stir in the grated turmeric, ginger, and minced garlic. Cook for another 1–2 minutes until fragrant.
4. Add the sliced bell peppers, broccoli florets, and snap peas to the skillet. Stir-fry for about 5–6 minutes or until the vegetables are tender-crisp.
5. Drizzle the soy sauce over the stir-fry and mix well. Cook for another minute to heat through.
6. Remove from heat and serve the stir-fry over cooked rice or quinoa. Garnish with fresh cilantro.

Baked Spinach and Feta Pasta

Wellness Wonders: Benefits

This easy baked pasta uses spinach, a powerful antioxidant, and feta cheese, creating a creamy, satisfying dish with fewer inflammatory ingredients than typical cheese-based sauces.

Yield: 4 servings

Prep: 10 minutes

Cook: 25–32 minutes

Total Time: 35–42 minutes

Nutritional Information:

Cals	Carbs	Fat	Protein	Fiber
350	45g	15g	12g	3g

Ingredients:

- 8 oz (about 2 cups) pasta (penne or rotini work well)
- 2 cups fresh spinach
- 1 cup feta cheese, crumbled
- 1 cup cherry tomatoes, halved
- 1/4 cup grated Parmesan cheese
- 3 cloves garlic, minced
- 1/2 tsp dried oregano
- 1/2 tsp dried basil
- 2 tbsp olive oil
- salt and pepper to taste
- fresh parsley, chopped (for garnish, optional)

Instructions:

1. Preheat your oven to 375°F (190°C).
2. In a large pot, bring salted water to a boil. Add the pasta and cook according to package instructions until al dente. Drain and set aside.
3. In a large mixing bowl, combine the cooked pasta, fresh spinach, crumbled feta cheese, cherry tomatoes, minced garlic, dried oregano, dried basil, olive oil, salt, and pepper. Toss until all ingredients are well combined.
4. Pour the pasta mixture into a greased 9x13-inch baking dish. Spread it evenly.
5. Sprinkle the grated Parmesan cheese evenly over the top of the pasta.
6. Bake in the preheated oven for 20–25 minutes, or until the cheese is melted and the pasta is heated through.

7. Remove the baking dish from the oven and let it cool slightly. Garnish with fresh parsley if desired and serve warm.

Zucchini Noodles With Pesto and Grilled Shrimp

Wellness Wonders: Benefits

This refreshing dish pairs anti-inflammatory zucchini noodles with omega-3-rich grilled shrimp and a basil pesto, offering a low-carb, nutrient-packed meal that supports heart health and reduces inflammation.

Yield: 4 servings

Prep: 15 minutes

Cook: 6–9 minutes

Total Time: 21–24 minutes

Nutritional Information:

Cals	Carbs	Fat	Protein	Fiber
330	14g	21g	23g	3g

Ingredients:

- **Pesto:**
    - 2 cups fresh basil leaves
    - 1/2 cup grated Parmesan cheese
    - 1/3 cup pine nuts or walnuts
    - 2 cloves garlic
    - salt (to taste)
    - 1/2 cup olive oil
- **Grilled Shrimp:**
    - 1 pound (450g) large shrimp, peeled and deveined
    - 2 tbsp olive oil
    - 2 cloves garlic, minced
    - salt and pepper (to taste)
- **Zucchini Noodles:**
    - 2 tbsp olive oil
    - 4 medium zucchinis, spiralized into noodles
    - salt and pepper (to taste)

Instructions:

1. In a food processor, combine the basil, Parmesan cheese, pine nuts, garlic, and salt. Pulse until finely chopped. With the processor running, slowly drizzle in the olive oil until the pesto is smooth. Taste and adjust seasoning, if needed. Set aside.
2. In a bowl, combine the shrimp, olive oil, minced garlic, salt, and pepper. Toss until the shrimp are well coated.

3. Preheat a grill pan over medium-high heat. Grill the shrimp for about 2–3 minutes per side, or until the color is pink and opaque. Remove from the grill.

4. In a large skillet, heat the olive oil over medium heat. Add the spiralized zucchini noodles, season with salt and pepper, and sauté for about 2–3 minutes until just tender but still al dente.

5. Remove the skillet from heat. Mix the pesto into the noodles and toss well to combine.

6. Divide the zucchini noodles among plates and top with the grilled shrimp. Serve immediately.

Concluding Thoughts

Each of the dinners featured in this chapter are great for relieving pain and inflammation due to being rich in omega-3 fatty acids and antioxidants. Chapter 5, is all about snacks and sides to stop us reaching for junk food when the cravings hit!

Chapter 6:

Snacks and Sides

Turmeric Roasted Chickpeas

Wellness Wonders: Benefits

These crunchy chickpeas are infused with anti-inflammatory turmeric, offering a protein-rich, fiber-packed snack that supports immune health and promotes digestive wellness.

Yield: 4 servings

Prep: 10 minutes

Cook: 25–30 minutes

Total Time: 35–35 minutes

Nutritional Information:

Cals	Carbs	Fat	Protein	Fiber
140	22g	5g	6g	6g

Ingredients:

- 1 can (15 oz) chickpeas
- 1 tbsp olive oil
- 1 tsp turmeric powder
- 1 tsp cumin
- 1/2 tsp paprika
- 1/2 tsp garlic powder
- salt and pepper (to taste)
- optional: Fresh lemon juice for serving

Instructions:

1. Preheat your oven to 400°F (200°C).
2. After rinsing and draining the chickpeas, pat them dry with a paper towel. Remove any loose skins for extra crunch.
3. In a mixing bowl, combine the chickpeas, olive oil, turmeric powder, cumin, paprika, garlic powder, salt, and pepper. Toss until the chickpeas are evenly coated.
4. Spread the seasoned chickpeas in a single layer on a baking sheet lined with parchment paper.
5. Bake in the preheated oven for 25–30 minutes, stirring halfway through, until the chickpeas are crispy and golden brown.
6. Remove from the oven and let them cool slightly. If desired, squeeze fresh lemon juice over the roasted chickpeas for added flavor. Serve warm or at room temperature as a snack or salad topping.

Avocado Hummus With Carrot Sticks

Wellness Wonders: Benefits

This creamy dip combines fiber-rich chickpeas with anti-inflammatory avocado, creating a nutrient-dense snack that supports heart health and pairs perfectly with antioxidant-packed carrot sticks for an immune-boosting bite.

Yield: 4 servings

Prep: 10 minutes

Cook: N/A

Total Time: 10 minutes

Nutritional Information:

Cals	Carbs	Fat	Protein	Fiber
150	18g	7g	5g	5g

Ingredients:

- **Avocado Hummus:**
  - 1 ripe avocado, peeled and pitted
  - 1 can (15 oz) chickpeas, rinsed and drained
  - 1/4 cup tahini
  - 2 tbsp lemon juice
  - 1–2 cloves garlic, minced
  - 1/2 tsp cumin
  - salt and pepper (to taste)
  - 2–3 tbsp water (to reach desired consistency)
- **Carrot Sticks:**
  - 4 large carrots

Instructions:

1. In a food processor, combine the avocado, chickpeas, tahini, lemon juice, minced garlic, cumin, salt, and pepper.
2. Process the mixture until smooth, scraping down the sides as needed. If the hummus is too thick, add water 1 tablespoon at a time until the desired consistency is reached.
3. Taste the hummus and adjust seasoning with additional salt, pepper, or lemon juice if desired.
4. While the hummus is blending, cut the large carrots into sticks for dipping.
5. Transfer the avocado hummus to a serving bowl and arrange the carrot sticks around it. Enjoy as a healthy snack or appetizer.

Spinach and Mushroom Mini Frittatas

Wellness Wonders: Benefits

Spinach is rich in vitamins A, C, and K, as well as iron and calcium, supporting immune function, skin health, and bone density. Mushrooms provide antioxidants, promote heart health, and contribute to weight management. Together, they create a protein-packed dish when combined with eggs, which can boost satiety and muscle health.

Yield: 12 mini frittatas

Prep: 10 minutes

Cook: 25–29 minutes

Total Time: 35–39 minutes

Nutritional Information:

Cals	Carbs	Fat	Protein	Fiber
90	2g	6g	7g	0.5g

Ingredients:

- olive oil or cooking spray, for greasing the muffin tin
- 1/4 cup onion, diced
- 1 cup mushrooms, diced (button or cremini)
- 1 cup fresh spinach, chopped
- 2 cloves garlic, minced
- salt and pepper, to taste
- 6 large eggs
- 1/4 cup milk
- 1/2 cup shredded cheese (cheddar or feta)
- a handful of cherry tomatoes, for garnish

Instructions:

1. Preheat your oven to 350°F (175°C).
2. Grease a muffin tin with olive oil or cooking spray to prevent sticking.
3. In a skillet over medium heat, add a small amount of olive oil. Once hot, add the diced onion and cook until translucent, about 2–3 minutes. Add the mushrooms and cook until softened, about 3–4 minutes. Add the chopped spinach and minced garlic, cooking until the spinach is wilted. Season with salt and pepper, then remove from heat.
4. In a large mixing bowl, whisk together the eggs and milk until well combined. Season with salt and pepper to taste.
5. Stir in the sautéed vegetables and shredded cheese into the egg mixture.
6. Pour the egg and vegetable mixture into the prepared muffin tin, filling each cup about 3/4 full.

7. Bake in the preheated oven for approximately 18–20 minutes, or until the frittatas are set and a toothpick inserted in the center comes out clean.

8. Allow the mini frittatas to cool in the pan for a few minutes before gently removing them. Serve warm or store in the refrigerator for later.

9. Garnish with a handful of cherry tomatoes when serving.

Peanut Butter Energy Balls

Wellness Wonders: Benefits

These bite-sized snacks combine protein-rich peanut butter with fiber-packed oats and anti-inflammatory flaxseeds, offering a satisfying, energizing treat that supports heart health and stabilizes blood sugar.

Yield: 12 servings (approximately 1 energy ball each)

Prep: 10 minutes

Cook: N/A

Chill: 30 minutes

Total Time: 40 minutes

Nutritional Information:

Cals	Carbs	Fat	Protein	Fiber
150	18g	7g	4g	2g

Ingredients:

- 1 cup old-fashioned oats
- 1/2 cup creamy peanut butter
- 1/3 cup honey
- 1/4 cup ground flaxseed
- 1/2 cup chocolate chips
- 1/2 tsp vanilla extract
- a pinch of salt

Instructions:

1. In a large mixing bowl, combine the old-fashioned oats, peanut butter, honey, ground flaxseed, chocolate chips, vanilla extract, and salt.
2. Use a spatula or your hands to mix all the ingredients together until fully combined. If the mixture is too dry, add a little more peanut butter or honey to reach the desired consistency.
3. Once the mixture is well combined, use your hands to scoop out small portions (about 1 tablespoon each) and roll them into balls.
4. Place the energy balls on a baking sheet or plate lined with parchment paper. Refrigerate for at least 30 minutes to firm up.
5. Once chilled, transfer the energy balls to an airtight container. They can be stored in the refrigerator for up to one week or in the freezer for longer storage.
6. Enjoy them as a quick snack, pre-workout fuel, or a healthy dessert!

Dark Chocolate Trail Mix

Wellness Wonders: Benefits

This nutrient-dense mix combines antioxidant-rich dark chocolate with heart-healthy nuts and anti-inflammatory seeds, creating a satisfying snack that supports brain health and provides sustained energy.

Yield: 6 servings

Prep: 5 minutes

Cook: N/A

Total Time: 5 minutes

Nutritional Information:

Cals	Carbs	Fat	Protein	Fiber
210	23g	12g	5g	3g

Ingredients:

- 1 cup raw almonds
- 1 cup cashews
- 1 cup walnuts
- 1/2 cup dried cranberries
- 1/2 cup raisins
- 1 cup dark chocolate chips (70% cocoa or higher)
- 1/2 cup pumpkin seeds (pepitas)
- 1/2 tsp sea salt
- 1 tsp cinnamon

Instructions:

1. In a large mixing bowl, combine the raw almonds, cashews, walnuts, dried cranberries, raisins, dark chocolate chips, and pumpkin seeds.
2. Sprinkle in the sea salt and cinnamon. Toss all the ingredients together until well mixed.
3. Divide the trail mix into individual portions or store in an airtight container.
4. Enjoy as a snack on the go, during hikes, or as a healthy treat!

Concluding Thoughts

All of the above recipes will help with not only curbing your cravings but reducing inflammation throughout your body too! Next, we're moving on to my favorite meal of the day—dessert!

Chapter 7:

Delicious Desserts

Avocado Brownies

Wellness Wonders: Benefits
Creamy avocado provides healthy fats in these rich, fudgy brownies, and cocoa adds an extra boost of antioxidants.

Yield: 12 bars

Prep: 10 minutes

Cook: 20–25 minutes

Chill: 10–15 minutes

Total Time: 40–50 minutes

Nutritional Information:

Cals	Carbs	Fat	Protein	Fiber
160	22g	7g	4g	4g

Ingredients:

- 1 ripe avocado, peeled and pitted
- 1/2 cup creamy peanut butter
- 1/2 cup honey
- 1 tsp vanilla extract
- 1/2 cup unsweetened cocoa powder
- 1/2 tsp baking powder
- 1/4 tsp salt
- 1/2 cup dark chocolate chips

Instructions:

1. Preheat your oven to 350°F (175°C). Grease an 8x8-inch baking dish or line it with parchment paper.
2. In a mixing bowl, mash the ripe avocado until smooth. You can use a fork or a food processor for this.
3. To the mashed avocado, add the peanut butter, honey, and vanilla extract. Mix until well combined and smooth.
4. In a separate bowl, whisk together the cocoa powder, baking powder, and salt. Slowly add the dry mixture to the wet mixture, stirring until just combined.
5. Fold in the dark chocolate chips gently.
6. Pour the brownie batter into the prepared baking dish and spread it evenly.

7. Bake in the preheated oven for 20–25 minutes, or until a toothpick inserted into the center comes out mostly clean (a few moist crumbs are fine).

8. Allow the brownies to cool in the pan for about 10-15 minutes before slicing into squares.

Almond Flour Pancakes With Berries

Wellness Wonders: Benefits

Almond flour is high in vitamin E and healthy fats, both beneficial for reducing inflammation. Adding berries like blueberries or strawberries provides antioxidants that combat free radicals.

Yield: 4 servings (about 8 pancakes)

Prep: 15 minutes

Cook: 40 minutes–56 minutes

Total Time: 55–71 minutes

Nutritional Information:

Cals	Carbs	Fat	Protein	Fiber
250	16g	18g	10g	4g

Ingredients:

- 1 cup almond flour
- 2 large eggs
- 1/4 cup almond milk or other milk choice
- 1 tbsp honey
- 1 tsp baking powder
- 1/2 tsp vanilla extract
- a pinch of salt
- fresh berries (blueberries, strawberries, or raspberries), for serving
- coconut oil, for cooking

Instructions:

1. In a large mixing bowl, combine the almond flour, baking powder, and salt. Mix well to ensure the baking powder is evenly distributed.
2. In a separate bowl, whisk together the eggs, milk, honey, and vanilla extract until smooth.
3. Pour the wet ingredients into the dry ingredients. Mix until just combined and take care not to overmix the batter, it should be thick.
4. Heat a non-stick skillet or griddle over medium heat and add a small amount of coconut oil to coat the surface.
5. Pour about 1/4 cup of batter for each pancake onto the skillet. Cook for about 3–4 minutes, or until bubbles form on the surface and the edges look set. Flip and cook for an additional 2–3 minutes until golden brown on both sides.
6. Repeat the process with the remaining batter, adding more oil to the skillet as needed.
7. Stack the pancakes on plates and top with fresh berries. You can also drizzle extra honey or maple syrup on top if desired.

Lemon Blueberry Cheesecake Bars

Wellness Wonders: Benefits

Made with cashews and blueberries, these no-bake bars are creamy, dairy-free, and packed with anti-inflammatory nutrients.

Yield: 12 bars

Prep: 10 minutes

Cook: 33—40 minutes

Chill: 30 minutes

Set: 2—4 hours

Total Time: 3 hours 13 minutes—5 hours 20 minutes

Nutritional Information:

Cals	Carbs	Fat	Protein	Fiber
190	22g	10g	3g	1g

Ingredients:

- **Crust:**
  - 1 1/2 cups graham cracker crumbs
  - 1/4 cup granulated sugar
  - 1/2 cup unsalted butter, melted
- **Cheesecake Filling:**
  - 16 oz (450g) cream cheese, softened
  - 1/2 cup granulated sugar
  - 2 large eggs
  - 1/4 cup sour cream
  - 2 tbsp lemon juice
  - 1 tsp lemon zest
  - 1 cup fresh or frozen blueberries

Instructions:

1. Preheat your oven to 325°F (160°C). Line an 8x8-inch baking dish with parchment paper, leaving some overhang for easy removal later.
2. In a medium bowl, combine the graham cracker crumbs, sugar, and melted butter. Mix until the crumbs are evenly coated. Press the mixture firmly into the bottom of the prepared baking dish to form an even crust.
3. Bake the crust in the preheated oven for about 8–10 minutes until lightly golden. Remove from the oven and let it cool slightly.

4. In a large mixing bowl, beat the softened cream cheese and sugar together using an electric mixer until smooth and creamy. Add the eggs one at a time, giving everything a good mix after each one.
5. Add the sour cream, lemon juice, lemon zest, and mix until fully incorporated.
6. Gently fold in the blueberries and be careful not to crush them.
7. Pour the cheesecake filling over the cooled crust and spread it evenly.
8. Bake in the preheated oven for 25–30 minutes, or until the center is set and only slightly jiggly.
9. Remove from the oven and allow to cool at room temperature for about 30 minutes. Then, refrigerate for at least 2–4 hours until fully chilled and set.
10. Once set, lift the cheesecake out of the pan using the parchment overhang. Cut into squares and serve chilled.

Sweet Potato Pie

Wellness Wonders: Benefits

Using naturally sweet and fiber-rich sweet potatoes, this pie is an ideal dessert with warming spices like cinnamon and ginger.

Yield: 8 servings

Prep: 20 minutes

Chill: 30 minutes

Cook: 1 hour 5–10 minutes

Cool: 30 minutes

Total Time: 2 hour 25–30 minutes

Nutritional Information:

Cals	Carbs	Fat	Protein	Fiber
230	32g	10g	3g	3g

Ingredients:

- **Pie Crust:**
    - 1 1/4 cups all-purpose flour
    - 1/2 tsp salt
    - 1/2 cup unsalted butter, chilled and diced
    - 1/4 cup ice water
- **Sweet Potato Filling:**
    - 2 cups cooked sweet potatoes (about 2 medium sweet potatoes)
    - 3/4 cup granulated sugar
    - 1/2 cup almond milk
    - 2 large eggs
    - 1 tsp vanilla extract
    - 1 tsp ground cinnamon
    - 1/2 tsp ground nutmeg
    - 1/4 tsp ground ginger
    - 1/4 tsp salt

Instructions:

1. In a mixing bowl, combine the flour and salt. Add the chilled butter and mix using a pastry cutter or your fingers until the mixture resembles coarse crumbs.
2. Stir in the ice water, a tablespoon at a time, until the dough comes together. Form the dough into a ball, flatten it into a disk, wrap in plastic wrap, and refrigerate for at least 30 minutes.

3. Preheat your oven to 350°F (175°C).

4. In a large mixing bowl, combine the cooked sweet potatoes, sugar, milk, eggs, vanilla extract, cinnamon, nutmeg, ginger, and salt. Use a mixer or a fork to mash and combine the mixture until smooth and creamy.

5. On a floured surface, roll out the chilled dough to fit a 9-inch pie dish. Carefully transfer the dough to the dish, trimming any excess hanging over the edges. Use a fork to gently prick the bottom of the crust to stop it bubbling while cooking.

6. Bake the pie crust in the preheated oven for about 10 minutes until lightly golden. Remove from the oven and allow to cool slightly.

7. Pour the sweet potato filling into the pre-baked pie crust, smoothing the top with a spatula.

8. Bake in the oven for 55–60 minutes, or until the filling is set and a knife inserted in the center comes out clean.

9. Remove from the oven and let the pie cool on a wire rack for at least 30 minutes before slicing. Serve warm or at room temperature.

Tart Cherry Nice Cream

Wellness Wonders: Benefits

A dairy-free, low-sugar "nice cream" made from tart cherries and bananas. This frozen dessert is not only refreshing but also contains melatonin and antioxidants that support inflammation reduction.

Yield: 2 servings

Prep: 15 minutes

Cook: N/A

Optional Freezing: 1–2 hours

Total Time: 15 minutes (or with optional freezing) 1–2 hours 15 minutes

Nutritional Information:

Cals	Carbs	Fat	Protein	Fiber
150	35g	Negligible	1.5g	3g

Ingredients:

- 2 ripe bananas, sliced and frozen
- 1 cup tart cherries (fresh, pitted)
- 1 tbsp maple syrup (adjust for sweetness)
- 1/2 tsp vanilla extract
- splash of almond milk (optional)

Instructions:

1. In a food processor or high-speed blender, combine the frozen banana slices and tart cherries. Add maple syrup (adjust for sweetness) and vanilla extract.
2. Blend the mixture on high speed until it becomes creamy and smooth, scraping down the sides as needed. You may need to stop occasionally to scrape down the sides to ensure everything is well mixed.
3. If the mixture is too thick, you can add a splash of almond milk to help blend it better. Blend again until smooth.
4. You can serve the nice cream immediately for a soft-serve consistency. For a firmer texture, transfer it to an airtight container and freeze for about 1–2 hours.
5. If you chose to freeze it, allow the nice cream to sit at room temperature for a few minutes before scooping. Serve in bowls or cones and enjoy!

Concluding Thoughts

The desserts featured in this chapter prove that healthy eating can still provide a deliciously sweet punch and will ensure you're able to fight off sugar cravings. Next, we're going to be throwing together some gorgeous anti-inflammatory smoothies!

Chapter 8:

Sumptuous Smoothies

Who doesn't love a delicious smoothie? These options are easily thrown together in your blender and provide a fantastic way to fight inflammation!

Green Detox Smoothie With Kale and Ginger

Wellness Wonders: Benefits

Kale is rich in antioxidants and vitamins, and ginger is known for its anti-inflammatory properties.

Yield: 2 servings

Prep: 10 minutes

Cook: N/A

Total Time: 10 minutes

Nutritional Information:

Cals	Carbs	Fat	Protein	Fiber
180	36g	3g	4g	6g

Ingredients:

- 2 cups kale, washed, stems removed, and leaves chopped
- 1 banana
- 1 cup pineapple chunks (fresh or frozen)
- 1/2-inch piece of fresh ginger, peeled and grated (adjust to taste)
- 1 tbsp chia seeds
- 1 cup coconut water
- juice of 1/2 lemon
- ice cubes (optional, if using fresh fruit)
- optional garnish: Slice of lemon or fresh mint

Instructions:

1. In a blender, add the chopped kale, banana, pineapple chunks, grated ginger, chia seeds, coconut water, and lemon juice.
2. Blend on high speed until the mixture is smooth and creamy. If it's too thick, add a little extra coconut water and blend again.
3. If you prefer a colder smoothie, add a few ice cubes and blend until well combined.

4. Taste the smoothie and adjust sweetness or ginger level if desired by adding more banana or ginger, then blend again.

5. Pour the smoothie into glasses and enjoy immediately. Optionally garnish with a slice of lemon or a sprig of fresh mint.

Berry Antioxidant Smoothie With Almond Milk

Wellness Wonders: Benefits

The rich presence of berries are high in antioxidants like flavonoids that reduce inflammation. Almond milk provides healthy fats and vitamin E, which also contribute to reducing inflammation.

Yield: 2 servings

Prep: 10 minutes

Cook: N/A

Total Time: 10 minutes

Nutritional Information:

Cals	Carbs	Fat	Protein	Fiber
150	30g	4g	3g	6g

Ingredients:

- 1 cup mixed berries (rinsed, fresh or frozen; strawberries, blueberries, raspberries, blackberries)
- 1 banana (fresh or frozen)
- 1 cup almond milk (unsweetened)
- 1 tbsp chia seeds
- 1 tbsp honey (adjust to taste)
- 1/2 tsp vanilla extract
- ice cubes (optional, if using fresh fruit)

Instructions:

1. In a blender, add the mixed berries, banana, almond milk, chia seeds, honey, and vanilla extract.

2. Blend on high speed until the mixture is smooth and creamy. If the smoothie is too thick for your preference, add a little more almond milk and blend again.

3. If you prefer a colder smoothie, add a few ice cubes and blend until well combined.

4. Taste the smoothie and adjust sweetness if desired by adding more honey, then blend again.

5. Pour the smoothie into glasses and enjoy immediately. Optionally, garnish with a few whole berries on top.

Golden Milk Smoothie With Turmeric and Cinnamon

Wellness Wonders: Benefits

This creamy smoothie is anti-inflammatory due to the presence of turmeric, which contains curcumin, a compound known for its powerful anti-inflammatory properties. Cinnamon also has anti-inflammatory effects, making this smoothie beneficial for reducing inflammation in the body.

Yield: 2 servings

Prep: 10 minutes

Cook: N/A

Total Time: 10 minutes

Nutritional Information:

Cals	Carbs	Fat	Protein	Fiber
210	29g	8g	5g	3g

Ingredients:

- 1 banana (fresh or frozen)
- 1 cup almond milk
- 1 tbsp almond butter
- 1 tsp ground turmeric
- 1/2 tsp ground cinnamon
- 1 tbsp honey (adjust to taste)
- 1/4 tsp black pepper
- 1/2 tsp vanilla extract
- ice cubes (optional, if using fresh ingredients)

- optional garnish: A pinch of cinnamon or turmeric

Instructions:

1. In a blender, add the banana, almond milk, almond butter, ground turmeric, ground cinnamon, honey, black pepper, and vanilla extract.
2. Blend on high speed until the mixture is smooth and creamy. If it's too thick, add a splash more almond milk and blend again.
3. If you prefer a colder smoothie, add a few ice cubes and blend until well combined.
4. Taste the smoothie and adjust sweetness if desired by adding more honey, then blend again.
5. Pour the smoothie into glasses and enjoy immediately. Optionally, sprinkle a pinch of cinnamon or turmeric on top for garnish.

Peanut Butter and Banana Energy Smoothie

Wellness Wonders: Benefits

Peanut butter contains healthy fats and proteins, while bananas are rich in potassium and antioxidants which can help reduce inflammation.

Yield: 2 servings

Prep: 5 minutes

Cook: N/A

Total Time: 5 minutes

Nutritional Information:

Cals	Carbs	Fat	Protein	Fiber
350	45g	15g	10g	6g

Ingredients:

- 2 ripe bananas (fresh or frozen)
- 1 cup almond milk
- 1/4 cup creamy peanut butter
- 1 tbsp honey
- 1 tbsp chia seeds

- a pinch of cinnamon
- ice cubes (optional, if using fresh bananas)

Instructions:

1. In a blender, add the bananas, almond milk, peanut butter, honey, chia seeds, and a pinch of cinnamon.
2. Blend on high speed until the mixture is smooth and creamy. If the smoothie is too thick for your liking, you can add a little more almond milk and blend again.
3. If you prefer a colder smoothie, add a few ice cubes and blend until well combined.
4. Taste the smoothie and adjust sweetness if desired by adding more honey, then blend again.
5. Pour the smoothie into glasses and enjoy immediately. Optionally, you can drizzle a little extra peanut butter on top or sprinkle with some chia seeds for garnish.

Pineapple and Coconut Immune-Boosting Smoothie

Wellness Wonders: Benefits

Pineapple contains bromelain, an enzyme known for its anti-inflammatory properties, while coconut provides healthy fats that support overall immune function.

Yield: 2 servings

Prep: 5 minutes

Cook: N/A

Total Time: 5 minutes

Nutritional Information:

Cals	Carbs	Fat	Protein	Fiber
200	38g	3g	5g	5g

Ingredients:

- 1 cup fresh or frozen pineapple chunks
- 1 ripe banana (fresh or frozen)
- 1 cup coconut milk
- 1/2 cup Greek yogurt

- 1 tbsp chia seeds
- 1 tbsp honey
- a handful of spinach
- ice cubes (optional, if using fresh fruit)

Instructions:

1. In a blender, add the pineapple chunks, banana, coconut milk, Greek yogurt, chia seeds, honey, and spinach.
2. Blend on high speed until the mixture is smooth and creamy. If the smoothie is too thick for your preference, add a little more coconut water or milk and blend again.
3. If you want a colder smoothie, add a few ice cubes and blend until well combined.
4. Taste the smoothie and adjust sweetness if desired by adding more honey, then blend again.
5. Pour the smoothie into glasses and enjoy immediately. Garnish with a slice of pineapple or a sprinkle of chia seeds, if desired.

Concluding Thoughts

The blended anti-inflammatory ingredients in each of the delicious smoothies in this chapter allow for quick nutrient absorption, making them a great addition to our daily dietary routines!

Those of you that aren't too keen on smoothies will be pleased to know that our next chapter is all about anti-inflammatory teas and drinks—let's go!

Chapter 9:

Tantalizing Teas and Divine Drinks

We're going to round off our recipe chapters with some teas and drinks that are fantastic for fighting inflammation without filling us up or needing lots of prior preparation.

Green Tea With Ginger

Wellness Wonders: Benefits

Green tea contains antioxidants called catechins, which reduce inflammation. Ginger has anti-inflammatory properties that can help alleviate pain and improve overall health. Together, they create a powerful combination that may lower inflammation in the body.

Yield: 2 servings

Prep: 5 minutes

Cook: 5 minutes

Total Time: 10 minutes

Nutritional Information:

Cals	Carbs	Fat	Protein	Fiber
2	Negligible	Negligible	Negligible	Negligible

Ingredients:

- 2 cups water
- 2 green tea bags
- 1-inch piece of fresh ginger, peeled and sliced
- 1–2 tbsp honey (optional, to taste)
- optional garnish: Lemon slices, fresh mint leaves

Instructions:

1. In a small saucepan, bring 2 cups of water to a boil over medium-high heat.
2. Once the water reaches a boil, add the sliced fresh ginger to the water. Reduce heat and let it simmer for about 5 minutes to allow the ginger to infuse the water.
3. Remove the saucepan from heat and add the green tea bags. Let it steep for about 3–5 minutes, depending on your taste preference. The longer it steeps, the stronger the flavor.
4. If you prefer a sweeter tea, add honey to taste. Stir well until dissolved.
5. Remove the tea bags.

6. Garnish with lemon slices and fresh mint leaves, if desired.
7. Serve hot and enjoy your refreshing Green Tea With Ginger!

Turmeric Golden Milk

Wellness Wonders: Benefits

Turmeric contains curcumin, which has anti-inflammatory properties.

Yield: 2 servings

Prep: 5 minutes

Cook: 10 minutes

Total Time: 15 minutes

Nutritional Information:

Cals	Carbs	Fat	Protein	Fiber
90	10g	4g	2g	1g

Ingredients:

- 2 cups almond milk
- 1 tsp ground turmeric
- 1/2 tsp ground cinnamon
- 1/4 tsp ground ginger
- 1 tbsp honey (optional)
- a pinch of black pepper
- 1 tsp coconut oil
- optional garnish: A dash of cinnamon

Instructions:

1. In a small saucepan, pour in the almond milk. Heat over medium heat, stirring occasionally, until it is warm but not boiling.
2. Once the milk is warm, add the ground turmeric, cinnamon, ginger, and black pepper. Whisk the mixture until the spices are well combined and there are no lumps.

3. If desired, stir in the honey to sweeten the golden milk. Add coconut oil.

4. Allow the mixture to simmer gently for about 5 minutes, stirring occasionally. This will help to infuse the flavors and enhance the health benefits of the spices.

5. Serve the golden milk warm in mugs, sprinkling them with a little cinnamon if you wish.

Lemon and Ginger Water

Wellness Wonders: Benefits

Lemon and Ginger Water is considered anti-inflammatory due to the presence of compounds in both lemon and ginger. Ginger contains gingerol, a powerful anti-inflammatory agent that can help reduce inflammation in the body. Lemon is rich in vitamin C and antioxidants, which may also aid in combating inflammation. Together, they create a drink that can support overall health and reduce inflammation.

Yield: 2 servings

Prep: 5 minutes

Cook: 5 minutes

Total Time: 10 minutes

Nutritional Information:

Cals	Carbs	Fat	Protein	Fiber
10	3g	Negligible	Negligible	Negligible

Ingredients:

- 2 cups water
- 1 lemon (juiced, plus additional slices for garnish)
- 1-inch piece of fresh ginger
- optional: Honey or maple syrup (to taste)

Instructions:

1. In a small saucepan, bring the water to a boil over medium-high heat. Alternatively, you can use filtered water at room temperature if you prefer it cold.

2. While the water is boiling, peel and slice the fresh ginger root into thin slices or grate it for a stronger flavor.

3. Once the water has boiled, remove it from heat and add the sliced or grated ginger. Let it steep for about 5 minutes to infuse the ginger flavor into the water.

4. Squeeze the juice of one lemon into the water, making sure to strain out any seeds.

5. If desired, add honey or maple syrup to taste, stirring until dissolved.

6. Pour the ginger-infused lemon water into glasses. If you like, you can add lemon slices for garnish.

7. Serve warm or allow it to cool and serve over ice.

Peppermint Tea

Wellness Wonders: Benefits

Peppermint Tea is considered anti-inflammatory due to the presence of compounds like rosmarinic acid and menthol, which can help reduce inflammation and soothe irritation in the body.

Yield: 2 servings

Prep: 5–7 minutes

Cook: 5 minutes

Total Time: 10–12 minutes

Nutritional Information:

Cals	Carbs	Fat	Protein	Fiber
10	3g	Negligible	Negligible	Negligible

Ingredients:

- 2 cups water
- 2 tbsp fresh peppermint leaves (or 2 peppermint tea bags)
- honey or sweetener of choice (optional)

Instructions:

1. In a small saucepan, bring 2 cups of water to a boil over medium-high heat.

2. If using fresh peppermint leaves, gently wash and pat them dry. You can slightly bruise them with a spoon to release more flavor.

3. Once the water is boiling, remove it from heat and add the fresh peppermint leaves directly to the water. Cover and let steep for about 5–7 minutes. If you're using tea bags, remove the boiling water

from heat and add the peppermint tea bags to the water. Cover and let steep for about 5–7 minutes as well.

4. If using fresh leaves, strain the tea into cups to remove the leaves. If using tea bags, simply remove the bags.
5. Add honey or your preferred sweetener to taste, stirring until dissolved.
6. Enjoy your Peppermint Tea hot. You can also let it cool and serve it over ice for a refreshing iced tea.

Hibiscus and Cinnamon Iced Tea

Wellness Wonders: Benefits

Hibiscus boasts powerful antioxidant properties that can significantly alleviate inflammation. Similarly, cinnamon is rich in anti-inflammatory compounds that may mitigate various risk factors linked to inflammation.

Yield: 4 servings

Prep: 10–15 minutes

Cook: 5 minutes

Chill: 1–2 hours

Total Time: 1 hour 15 minutes–2 hours 20 minutes

Nutritional Information:

Cals	Carbs	Fat	Protein	Fiber
5	1g	Negligible	Negligible	Negligible

Ingredients:

- 4 cups water
- 1/2 cup dried hibiscus flowers
- 1 cinnamon stick
- 1/4 cup honey or maple syrup (adjust to taste)
- ice cubes
- optional garnish: Fresh mint leaves or lemon slices.

Instructions:

1. In a medium saucepan, bring the water to a boil over medium-high heat.
2. Once the water is boiling, remove it from heat and add the dried hibiscus flowers and the cinnamon stick.
3. Cover the saucepan and let the mixture steep for about 10–15 minutes. The longer you steep, the stronger the flavor will be.
4. After steeping, strain the mixture into a pitcher to remove the hibiscus flowers and cinnamon stick.
5. While the tea is still warm, stir in the honey or maple syrup until dissolved. Adjust sweetness to your preference.
6. Allow the tea to cool to room temperature, then refrigerate for at least 1–2 hours until chilled.
7. To serve, fill glasses with ice cubes, pour the chilled hibiscus and cinnamon tea over the ice, and garnish with fresh mint leaves or lemon slices if desired.

Concluding Thoughts

These drinks are refreshing ways of reducing inflammation, and can be made in batches to make things easier on your busiest days.

Question and Answer Time With Rosa

What are the essential steps for starting an anti-inflammatory diet? Begin by focusing on whole foods like fruits, vegetables, lean proteins, and healthy fats. Gradually reduce processed foods, added sugars, and refined grains.

How do I plan meals to avoid feeling overwhelmed? Start with simple recipes and plan meals for a few days at a time. Choose versatile ingredients, like leafy greens, berries, and whole grains, that you can use in multiple meals.

What are quick anti-inflammatory foods I can incorporate daily? Berries, leafy greens, nuts, seeds, olive oil, and spices like turmeric and ginger are easy to add to meals and they are packed with anti-inflammatory benefits.

How do I keep my meals affordable on an anti-inflammatory diet? Buy seasonal produce, shop bulk for grains and nuts, and choose frozen fruits and vegetables when possible. Look for budget-friendly proteins like beans, lentils, and canned fish.

What are easy substitutions for common inflammatory foods? Try swapping refined grains for whole grains (e.g., brown rice instead of white rice), vegetable oil for olive oil, and red meat for fish or legumes.

How do I handle cravings for unhealthy, processed foods? Keep healthy snacks like nuts, hummus with veggies, or fruit on hand to satisfy cravings. Experiment with anti-inflammatory alternatives to your favorite treats, like dark chocolate or fruit-based desserts.

What can I do when I'm eating out or traveling? Look for grilled or steamed dishes, choose vegetable sides, and avoid heavy sauces. Pack snacks like nuts or fruit when traveling to avoid unhealthy choices.

How can I maintain this lifestyle without feeling restricted? Focus on adding nourishing foods rather than cutting things out. Try new recipes, explore different flavors, and allow yourself the occasional indulgence.

How do I make time for an anti-inflammatory diet with a busy schedule? Prep meals in bulk, cook double portions, or use a slow cooker to save time. Keep quick, easy staples like pre-washed greens, canned beans, and frozen veggies on hand.

What are some tips for dealing with social events or family gatherings? Offer to bring a dish to share and aim for balance. Focus on eating anti-inflammatory options when you can and remember it's okay to indulge occasionally.

How soon will I start to feel the benefits? Some people feel changes like increased energy within days, while others may take weeks to notice reduced inflammation symptoms. Consistency is key.

What should I do if I get off track? Don't be hard on yourself. Simply start fresh with your next meal, focusing on whole, anti-inflammatory foods. Remember, it's a journey, and progress is what matters.

Conclusion

Embarking on an anti-inflammatory journey is more than just a dietary change—it's a lifestyle shift that opens doors to improved health and wellness. You have spent time learning about the powerful effects of inflammation reduction through food, understanding its impact not only on your physical health but also on how you feel day to day. Now, as you stand at the crossroads of continuing this path, it is essential to look back at what you have achieved and gaze forward with excitement and confidence.

Transitioning to an anti-inflammatory diet is akin to embracing a new mindset. It requires commitment, but the benefits are truly transformative. You have discovered foods that act as allies in fighting inflammation: colorful fruits, vibrant vegetables, omega-rich fish, and nutrient-packed spices like turmeric and ginger. These are not just ingredients; they are tools that help you reclaim control over your well-being. By making thoughtful choices about what you eat, you are sending powerful signals to your body to reduce inflammation, potentially alleviating symptoms of chronic diseases and promoting overall health.

Remember those first steps you took? Perhaps it was trying a new recipe, swapping out processed options for natural ones, or simply reading nutritional labels more closely. Though they might have seemed daunting initially, each step was significant in steering you toward a healthier version of yourself. It is crucial to celebrate these victories, no matter how small they seem, because they have paved the way for sustained change. As you continue this journey, keep experimenting and discovering what works best for you. Each body is unique, and your path will be distinctly yours.

The science behind why reducing inflammation is beneficial is both fascinating and compelling. Chronic inflammation has been linked to numerous health issues, from joint pain and fatigue to more severe conditions like heart disease and diabetes. By adopting an anti-inflammatory diet, you are taking proactive measures to safeguard against these complications. Food is medicine—never underestimate the power of simple, everyday choices in creating profound changes within your body.

In addition to tangible physical benefits, embracing this diet can foster a deeper connection to the food you consume and the world around you. Have you noticed how your palate has evolved? How foods you once overlooked now excite your taste buds with their freshness and flavors? This mindfulness extends beyond meals, encouraging a broader appreciation for the nourishment that fuels you. It is an ongoing journey about health and awareness, gratitude, and conscious living.

Life is unpredictable, and there will undoubtedly be moments when sticking to your anti-inflammatory habits feels challenging. Social gatherings, holidays, or hectic days might throw you off course. When these situations arise, practice self-compassion and flexibility. It is okay to indulge occasionally or adapt your plans to suit your circumstances. What is important is to maintain a balanced perspective and resume your practices. Remember, it's a marathon, not a sprint.

Your anti-inflammatory journey encompasses more than food—consider integrating complementary lifestyle changes that enhance its effects. Regular physical activity, adequate sleep, and stress management techniques like mindfulness and meditation all play crucial roles in maintaining low inflammation levels. Together, they create a holistic approach to health—one where mind, body, and spirit work harmoniously.

Reflecting on the road ahead, envision yourself firmly rooted in these habits and how they enrich your life. Imagine the energy to pursue passions, participate joyfully in activities, and engage fully with loved ones. This vision is within reach, attainable through dedication and informed choice. With every meal prepared and each bite savored, you are investing in a brighter, healthier future.

The personal growth accompanying this transformation should not be underestimated either. The resilience you build by persevering through challenges, along with the knowledge gained from exploring new foods and methods, all contribute to your sense of empowerment. Carry these lessons beyond the kitchen into other aspects of your life. The discipline and curiosity nurtured here can inspire positive changes across diverse areas.

As we wrap up our exploration of the anti-inflammatory diet and lifestyle, take a moment to appreciate how far you have come. You have embraced a new way of living, one that champions health and vitality. While the journey is not always linear, the rewards are plentiful, and the possibilities are endless.

Keep moving forward, staying open to learning and adapting. Trust in your ability to make impactful decisions that promote wellness and happiness. Celebrate your progress, share your journey with others, and embrace every opportunity for growth. You are armed with the knowledge, tools, and enthusiasm to thrive on this path and inspire others to embark on their healing journeys.

Your anti-inflammatory adventure is uniquely yours, filled with discovery, triumph, and transformation. Cherish each aspect of it, knowing that your commitment to nurturing your body is the gift that keeps on giving. Here's to continued success in your quest for health and a vibrant, fulfilling life!

Warm Regards,
Rosa James xxx

Your Anti-Inflammatory Journey Can Inspire Others!

Thank you for bringing ***The Anti-Inflammatory Diet Cookbook for Beginners*** into your kitchen. I hope the recipes and tips have made cooking easier, healthier, and more enjoyable for you. If this book has supported you on your journey to a healthier lifestyle, I'd be truly grateful if you could take a moment to leave a review. Your insights can inspire others to embrace an anti-inflammatory diet, and your experience may offer valuable guidance to those just starting out.

With gratitude,
Rosa James xxx

Author Bio

Rosa James is a culinary expert celebrated for her ability to craft delicious, nutritious dishes that accommodate a wide range of dietary needs. As a working mother with a family of varied preferences, Rosa understands the importance of creating quick, budget-friendly meals that don't compromise on taste or nutrition.

Diagnosed with celiac disease years ago, Rosa's journey to nourish and heal her body through food has been deeply personal. This experience led her to explore foods that support wellness, reduce inflammation, and restore energy. Her latest release, ***Anti-Inflammatory Diet Cookbook for Beginners***, embodies this journey by offering simple, science-backed recipes designed to boost energy, reduce inflammation, and promote overall health. The book is filled with diverse, budget-friendly recipes, making it easy for beginners to embrace an anti-inflammatory lifestyle.

Rosa's commitment to health and healing through food inspired her previous works, including ***The Quick and Easy Gluten-Free Air Fryer Cookbook*** and ***Mediterranean Diet Cookbook for Beginners***, which provide accessible, flavorful meals for gluten-free, vegetarian, and regular diets. Her journey of healing and adaptation has resulted in a collection of recipes that cater to various dietary needs and support whole-body wellness.

Whether you're exploring an anti-inflammatory diet, Mediterranean cooking, or need gluten-free options, Rosa's books offer practical, delicious solutions for every meal. Her love for desserts also shines through, with indulgent, easy-to-make treats that complement her savory dishes.

Rosa's cookbooks are more than just recipes; they're heartfelt guides for creating simple, wholesome meals that heal, nourish, and bring joy to the whole family.

References

Adjepong, E. (2024). *Cumin-Roasted carrots with dill yogurt.* EatingWell. https://www.eatingwell.com/recipe/7927880/cumin-roasted-carrots-with-dill-yogurt/

Avocado hummus. (n.d.). Just Veg. https://www.justveg.com.au/recipes/avocado-hummus/

Ball, J. (2020). *11 smoothie recipes to help keep inflammation at bay.* EatingWell. https://www.eatingwell.com/gallery/2061556/smoothie-recipes-anti-inflammation/

Ball, J. (2024). *28 anti-inflammatory recipes.* EatingWell. https://www.eatingwell.com/gallery/12952/anti-inflammatory-recipes/

The best breakfasts for sustained energy. (2024, June 10). SquashSkills. https://blog.squashskills.com/-/the-best-breakfasts-for-sustained-energy/

Brody, B. (2023). *Anti-Inflammatory diet: Foods to eat and avoid.* WebMD. https://www.webmd.com/diet/anti-inflammatory-diet-road-to-good-health

Bryan, L. (2023a). *Chocolate chia pudding.* Downshiftology. https://downshiftology.com/recipes/chocolate-chia-pudding/

Bryan, L. (2023b). *Golden milk (turmeric milk).* Downshiftology. https://downshiftology.com/recipes/turmeric-milk-dairy-free/

Casner, C. (2024). *Baked spinach & feta pasta.* EatingWell. https://www.eatingwell.com/recipe/7898240/baked-spinach-feta-pasta/

Chrichton-Stuart, C. (2022). *Anti-inflammatory meal plan: 26 recipes to try.* Medical News Today. https://www.medicalnewstoday.com/articles/322897

Christine. (2024, June 3). *Best recipe for picky eaters: The ultimate nutrient-boosted pancakes.* Foodology . https://foodologyfeedingtherapy.com/nutrient-packed-plain-pancakes-recipe-for-picky-eaters/

Coleman, E. (2024). *10 anti-inflammatory lunch ideas you can pack for work.* Rupa Health. https://www.rupahealth.com/post/anti-inflammatory-lunches

Ehsani, R. (2024). *The 7 best foods naturally high in melatonin, recommended by dietitians.* EatingWell. https://www.eatingwell.com/foods-with-melatonin-8663994

Ele. (n.d.). *Hibiscus iced tea recipe.* Food by Ele. https://foodbyele.com/hibiscus-iced-tea-recipe/

Ellis, S. (2021, July 4). *Balsamic grilled chicken salad.* The Culinary Compass. https://www.theculinarycompass.com/balsamic-grilled-chicken-salad/

Fisher, L. (2024). *10 anti-inflammatory breakfast ideas to start your morning on a healthy note.* Real Simple. https://www.realsimple.com/health/nutrition-diet/anti-inflammatory-breakfast

Foods that fight inflammation. (2024). Harvard Health Publishing. https://www.health.harvard.edu/staying-healthy/foods-that-fight-inflammation

Hobbs, H. (2024). *Which herbs can help reduce inflammation?* Healthline. https://www.healthline.com/health/osteoarthritis/turmeric-and-anti-inflammatory-herbs

Indian lentil curry with spinach. (n.d.). Glebe Kitchen. https://glebekitchen.com/indian-lentil-curry-with-spinach/

Juul, F., Vaidean, G., & Parekh, N. (2021). Ultra-processed foods and cardiovascular diseases: Potential mechanisms of action. *Advances in Nutrition, 12*(5). https://doi.org/10.1093/advances/nmab049

Kristina, & Mitja. (2017, November 17). *Crispy turmeric roasted chickpeas {vegan}*. Vibrant Plate; Vibrant Plate. https://www.vibrantplate.com/crispy-turmeric-roasted-chickpeas-vegan/

LeWine, H. (Ed.). (2024). *Foods that fight inflammation.* Harvard Health. https://www.health.harvard.edu/staying-healthy/foods-that-fight-inflammation

Lotts, L. (2017, April 27). *Individual spinach mushroom frittatas.* Garlic and Zest. https://www.garlicandzest.com/individual-spinach-mushroom-frittatas/

Loaiza, S. (2024, August 31). *Dark chocolate trail mix.* Six Sisters' Stuff. https://www.sixsistersstuff.com/recipe/dark-chocolate-trail-mix/

MacLean, H. (2022, January 13). *Tuna lettuce wraps recipe.* Tasting Table. https://www.tastingtable.com/658008/tuna-lettuce-wraps-recipe/

Mashhadi, N. S., Ghiasvand, R., Askari, G., Hariri, M., Darvishi, L., & Mofid, M. R. (2013). Anti-Oxidative and anti-inflammatory effects of ginger in health and physical activity: Review of current evidence. *International Journal of Preventive Medicine, 4*(1), S36-42. https://pmc.ncbi.nlm.nih.gov/articles/PMC3665023/

Mathis, A. (2024). *Tart cherry nice cream.* EatingWell. https://www.eatingwell.com/recipe/7916777/tart-cherry-nice-cream/

McCaffrey, K. (2024). *Pesto shrimp with zucchini noodles.* Slender Kitchen. https://www.slenderkitchen.com/recipe/pesto-shrimp-with-zucchini-noodles

McKenney, S. (2022, August 27). *Lemon blueberry cheesecake bars.* Sally's Baking Addiction. https://sallysbakingaddiction.com/lemon-blueberry-cheesecake-bars/

McMichael, C. (2024, January 25). *Vegan turmeric quinoa power bowls.* Jar of Lemons. https://www.jaroflemons.com/vegan-turmeric-quinoa-power-bowls/

Milesi, G., Rangan, A., & Grafenauer, S. (2022). Whole grain consumption and inflammatory markers: A systematic literature review of randomized control trials. *Nutrients, 14*(2), 374. https://doi.org/10.3390/nu14020374

Munuhe, N. (2023). *Healthy avocado brownies for A guilt-free treat.* BetterMe. https://betterme.world/articles/avocado-brownies/

Pajer, N. (2022, November 21). *9 superfoods to help you sleep.* AARP. https://www.aarp.org/health/healthy-living/info-2021/superfoods-for-sleep.html

Perry, M. G. (2024). *How to incorporate anti-inflammatory foods into your desserts.* Rupa Health. https://www.rupahealth.com/post/how-to-incorporate-anti-inflammatory-foods-into-your-desserts

Rath, L. (2022, December 8). *Omega-3 fatty acids for your health.* Arthritis Foundation. https://www.arthritis.org/health-wellness/treatment/complementary-therapies/supplements-and-vitamins/omega-3-fatty-acids-for-health

Sass, C. (2023, October 4). *9 health benefits of avocados.* Health. https://www.health.com/nutrition/avocado-health-benefits

6 delicious anti-inflammatory teas. (2023). Sjögren's Society of Canada. https://sjogrenscanada.org/living-with-sjgrens/recipes.html/article/2023/08/01/6-delicious-anti-inflammatory-teas

Spritzler, F. (2023). *What is an anti-inflammatory diet and how to follow it.* Healthline. https://www.healthline.com/nutrition/anti-inflammatory-diet-101

Stanford, J. (2024). *The top 6 anti-inflammatory spices to incorporate into your diet.* Rupa Health. https://www.rupahealth.com/post/the-top-6-anti-inflammatory-spices-to-incorporate-into-your-diet

Sweet potato pie. (2024). Allrecipes. https://www.allrecipes.com/recipe/12142/sweet-potato-pie-i/

3-Ingredient ginger lemon water. (n.d.). Minimalist Baker. Retrieved November 1, 2024, from https://minimalistbaker.com/3-ingredient-ginger-lemon-water/

Tristan Asensi, M., Napoletano, A., Sofi, F., & Dinu, M. (2023). Low-Grade inflammation and ultra-processed foods consumption: A review. *Nutrients, 15*(6), 1546. https://doi.org/10.3390/nu15061546

Valente, L. (2024). Peanut butter energy balls. *EatingWell.* https://www.eatingwell.com/recipe/275207/peanut-butter-energy-balls/

Wartenberg, L., & Spritzler, F. (2023). *Anti-Inflammatory foods to eat.* Healthline. https://www.healthline.com/nutrition/13-anti-inflammatory-foods#list

Wimberly, C. A. (2024). *16 easy anti-inflammatory lunches to make this week.* EatingWell. **https://www.eatingwell.com/easy-anti-inflammatory-lunch-recipes-8729424**

Printed in Great Britain
by Amazon